D0931569

Monetary Union in South America

Monetary Union in South America

Lessons from EMU

Edited by

Philip Arestis

Professor of Economics, The Levy Economics Institute of Bard College, USA

Luiz Fernando de Paula

Associate Professor of Economics, University of the State of Rio de Janeiro, Brazil

Edward Elgar

Cheltenham, UK • Northampton, MA, USA

Published by
Edward Elgar Publishing Limited
Glensanda House
Montpellier Parade
Cheltenham
Glos GL50 1UA
UK

Edward Elgar Publishing, Inc.
136 West Street
Suite 202
Northampton
Massachusetts 01060
USA

A catalogue record for this book
is available from the British Library

Library of Congress Cataloguing in Publication Data

Monetary union in South America : lessons from EMU / edited by Philip Arestis,
    Luiz Fernando de Paula.
        p. cm.
    Includes bibliographical references and index.
    1. Monetary unions—South America. 2. MERCOSUR (Organization).
    3. Monetary unions—Europe. 4. Economic and Monetary Union. I. Arestis, Philip,
    1941– II. Paula, Luiz Fernando de, 1959–

HG805.M66 2003
332.4'666'098—dc21   2003047760

ISBN 1 84376 057 6

Typeset by Cambrian Typesetters, Frimley, Surrey
Printed and bound in Great Britain by MPG Books Ltd, Bodmin, Cornwall

Contents

Figures

Tables

Contributors

Adriana Moreira Amado, Associate Professor of Economics, University of Brasília, Brazil.

Joaquim Pinto de Andrade, Professor of Economics, University of Brasília, Brazil.

Philip Arestis, Professor of Economics, The Levy Economics Institute of Baod College, USA.

José Maria Fanelli, Professor of Economics, University of Buenos Aires, and Senior Researcher at Center for the Study of State and Society (CEDES), Buenos Aires, Argentina.

Fernando Ferrari-Filho, Professor of Economics, Federal University of Rio Grande do Sul, Porto Alegre, Brazil.

John S. Flemming, Warden of Wadham College, Oxford, UK, and former Chief Economist of the European Bank for Reconstruction and Development.

Fabio Giambiagi, Economist at the Department of Economics, National Bank for Economic and Social Development (BNDES), Rio de Janeiro, Brazil.

Daniel Heymann, Senior Economist at the Economic Commission for Latin America and the Caribbean (ECLAC), Buenos Aires, and Professor of Economics at University of Buenos Aires, Argentina.

Arturo O'Connell, Director of the Master's Degree in Regional Integration at the University of Buenos Aires and Professor of International Finance at the University of Bologna, Buenos Aires, Argentina.

Luiz Fernando de Paula, Associate Professor of Economics, University of the State of Rio de Janeiro, Brazil.

Malcolm Sawyer, Professor of Economics, University of Leeds, UK.

Maria L. Falcão Silva, Associate Professor of Economics, University of Brasília, Brazil.

Luiz Afonso Simoens da Silva, Financial Director at Emurb – Empresa Municipal de Urbanizacao da Prefeitura de São Paulo, Brazil, and former economist at Central Bank of Brazil.

Rogério Studart, Economics Affairs Officer at the Economic Development Division of the Economic Commission for Latin America and the Caribbean (ECLAC), Santiago, Chile.

Hans-Michael Trautwein, Professor of International Economics at the Carl von Ossietzky University of Oldenburg, Germany.

Abbreviations

BIS	Bank for International Settlements
BNDES	National Bank for Economic and Social Development (Brazil)
CEDES	Center for the Study of State and Society (Argentina)
CEPAL	Comisión Económica para América Latina y el Caribe
CET	Common External Tariff
ECB	European Central Bank
ECLAC	Economic Commission for Latin America and the Caribbean
ECOFIN	European Council of Finance
EMU	European Monetary Union
ERR	Exchange Rate Regime
ESCB	European System of Central Banks
FDI	Foreign Direct Investment
FTA	Free Trade Area
FTAA	Free Trade Area of the Americas
HICP	Harmonized Index of Consumer Prices
IADB	Inter-American Development Bank
IFE	International Financial Environment
MERCOSUR	Mercado Común del Sur (Southern Common Market)
MPC	Monetary Policy Committee (UK)
NAFTA	North American Free Trade Area
NAIRU	Non-Accelerating Inflation Rate of Unemployment
OCA	Optimal Currency Area

Introduction

Philip Arestis and Luiz Fernando de Paula

In the last few years, the integration process in MERCOSUR (Mercado Común del Sur – the Southern Common Market) has been characterized by economic turbulence: the devaluation of the Brazilian currency in January 1999 resulted in spillover effects in the MERCOSUR area, more specifically in Argentina. The 2001–2 crisis in Argentina has had a destabilizing impact on macroeconomic indicators in the MERCOSUR countries, particularly in Brazil. Since Brazil has a floating exchange regime, the demand for hedging caused more and more devaluation of its currency, with serious impacts on Argentina's trade, as this country had until recently a fixed exchange regime. After the collapse of Argentina's system of convertibility, the extreme macroeconomic instability has been a serious restriction to any growth-oriented policy, and as a result the re-starting and developing of the integration process may be harmed. Consequently, the optimism about the integration process, which prevailed in the mid-1990s, when the intra-regional flows of goods were expanding at a very fast rate, was changed later into deep scepticism.

Taking these turbulences into consideration, a question arises: what is the future of MERCOSUR? This question can be answered in different ways. On the one hand there are those who argue that MERCOSUR should only become a free trade area. In this context, the final step of the integration process in MERCOSUR would be the Free Trade Area of the Americas scheduled for 2005. On the other hand, there are those who maintain that nothing less than a monetary union should be the solution. This argument makes the following three points in favour of a monetary union: (i) it would provide a new framework for economic management: a new way of conducting fiscal policy would be introduced, and it would modify the financial and monetary system of the member countries in a way that would make policies a great deal more effective; (ii) it would prevent new currency crises in the region; and (iii) it would stimulate a definitive economic integration among the countries of the bloc.[1] Other authors, however, claim that it is too early to think of a monetary union for MERCOSUR and are in favour of macroeconomic policy coordination among the country members of the bloc.[2]

Until recently, there had been indications that the integration process in MERCOSUR was going in the direction of a monetary union. The most important indicators were the following: in 1997 the former President of Argentina, Carlos Menen, proposed the 'dollarization' of MERCOSUR economies; in 1998 the annual regional summit of MERCOSUR indicated the possibility of having a single currency for the MERCOSUR countries; and in December 2000, the Presidents of the MERCOSUR countries declared their approval of macroeconomic convergence targets, namely inflation rate, fiscal deficit and net public debt. However, the adoption of a series of initiatives by Argentina's government during 2001, aiming to improve the country's competitiveness, seriously harmed imports of Brazilian products, and put at risk the very survival of the bloc. Since Argentina and Brazil had different currency regimes, and this difference was harming intra-MERCOSUR trade, the proposal of a MERCOSUR monetary union seemed to resurface in the debate as the unique solution to ensure the continuity of the bloc in the long term.

Economic and Monetary Union (EMU) is particularly relevant to the argument of the book, since it has been the main source of inspiration for the proposal to create a monetary union in MERCOSUR. It is for this reason that substantial reference is made to the EMU experience and institutional set-up in this book. The EMU experiment is also one of the very few examples of attempts of countries to unite under a common currency in the post-World War II era, an attribute that gives it added significance.

The principal aim of the book is to contribute to the academic debate on the future of MERCOSUR. Focusing on monetary unions, with particular reference to the EMU experience, and on the principles of economic policy coordination, the book addresses a number of questions, the most important ones being the following:

- Is it possible, or indeed desirable, to achieve monetary integration in MERCOSUR?
- What would the preconditions be for establishing such a union?
- What would the convergence criteria be for joining the monetary union?
- What are the expected economic consequences for the member countries of a MERCOSUR monetary union?
- Are there any other options than monetary union for MERCOSUR?
- What is the relevance of the EMU experience for MERCOSUR?

The book is divided into three parts for this purpose: the first part, entitled 'Lessons from the Euro and EMU for MERCOSUR', analyses the origins and dynamism of the monetary integration process in Europe, and the lessons for MERCOSUR. The second part, entitled 'MERCOSUR Macroeconomic Policy Coordination', contains contributions that present and discuss some of the necessary conditions for monetary union in MERCOSUR, such as the issue of macroeconomic convergence. The third part, entitled 'Exchange Rate Regimes and Monetary Dilemmas for MERCOSUR', discusses some specific macroeconomic issues concerning MERCOSUR and their impact on the future of the bloc, such as the external financial integration between Latin American economies and mature economies, and the recent collapse of Argentina's monetary regime. Whenever possible, technical detail has been kept to a minimum in the hope that this text will also be accessible to students. Alternative solutions to the problem under scrutiny are also discussed, such as macroeconomic policy coordination among the member countries without a monetary union in place. We hope that the eight chapters in this volume will give the reader a fresh perspective of the issues concerning macroeconomic coordination in MERCOSUR. As nations are becoming more and more inter-dependent, the need for a serious analysis of the macroeconomic conditions of economic and monetary integration becomes more pressing. We believe that the best way to discuss these issues is to expose the problem in hand to different approaches. We hope that this volume will contribute to the debate.

The opening chapter, by John Flemming, seeks to extract some lessons for MERCOSUR by focusing on the EMU experience. In his short note, Flemming first shows that since the process of EMU is not complete, it is too early to draw definitive conclusions from this experience. One of his fears for EMU is related to the possibility that its 'one-size-fits-all' monetary policy might leave some countries with untreated depression, but this has not happened. What has happened is a number of booms in certain peripheral countries, Ireland and Portugal in particular. But this peripheral boom has its counterpart in a relatively sluggish core of France, and particularly Germany. The effect of EMU on the peripheral countries has been virtually to diminish the risk premium reflected in their interest rates, since it eliminated the exchange rate risk. Since MERCOSUR does not have a core and a periphery, it is doubtful whether there is a useful lesson in this particular context. On the other hand, despite the ten-year-old single market and the two-year-old euro, the European market in corporate control is far from being free and unified. Germany has just blocked a directive on European takeovers. Consequently, mergers that create national champions do little to take advantage of any potential improvement in the scale/competition trade-off.

In the second chapter of the first part, Philip Arestis, Fernando Ferrari-Filho, Luiz Fernando de Paula and Malcolm Sawyer discuss whether the EMU mould of monetary union is appropriate and feasible for MERCOSUR. Three lessons are derived for MERCOSUR from the euro and the EMU experience. First, the adoption of the EMU model of monetary union would imply defla-tionary policies; there is little coordination of monetary and fiscal policies, and the deflationary policies, due essentially to the primacy of monetary policy over fiscal policy. The latter is guaranteed by the institutional structure and rules of the European System of Central Banks and the Stability and Growth Pact. Second, there is a dilemma of sequencing between political union and economic integration, since the formation of the EMU was not much influenced by economic convergence and political union considerations. Third, it is necessary to account seriously for the concerns of the optimal currency area (OCA) litera-ture, factor mobility and openness of markets, relative price flexibility, and fiscal transfers within the monetary union. These considerations appear to have played little role in the formation of the euro zone. In the case of MERCOSUR, the area has only minimally achieved some basic criteria defined by the OCA literature. The chapter concludes by suggesting that one lesson that can be extracted from the EMU experience is the avoidance of using this model as the benchmark for a possible MERCOSUR monetary union. Since the countries of MERCOSUR have more social problems than the countries of the EMU, the cost of adopting a MERCOSUR monetary union on the euro pattern would probably be greater than in the case of the EMU. So, it would be necessary to have much more flexible mechanisms of compensation in terms of fiscal transfers in order to tackle the socioeconomic problems of the MERCOSUR countries.

The second part of the book unfolds with a contribution by Fabio Giambiagi, who puts forward a proposal for a MERCOSUR monetary union in the long term. He adopts an encompassing approach to justify the long-term objective of currency unification among MERCOSUR countries. The theoret-ical advantages of a monetary union are: (i) more guarantees for stability ('tying one's hands'); (ii) stimulus for investment, related to the reduction of uncertainty and discretion; (iii) reduction of interest rates, as a consequence of the decrease in the exchange risk and regional risk; and (iv) elimination of transaction costs in the product, capital and labour markets. He presents further arguments in favour of a monetary union for MERCOSUR, such as the strengthening of the bloc in international negotiations, the advantages of the creation of an effective common market, and the creation of an intermediary regional power. MERCOSUR has some advantages over other regions that include democratic institutions, economies with capitalistic tradition, rela-tively sophisticated financial markets, recent economic stability, lack of conflicts (religious, ethnical, geographical, historical, external), and cultural identity. The next step in the argument describes the requirements for a single currency and the increasing homogeneity of the economies of the region. The chapter concludes by suggesting that this proposal can provide for a possible transitory agenda to 2002/2004 in order to reach a macroeconomic conver-gence in the region. This agenda includes an annual inflation target of 5.0 per cent, a 3.5 per cent ceiling on the ratio of the current account deficit to GDP, and a 3.5 per cent ceiling on the nominal public sector deficit to GDP. The chapter also emphasizes that currency unification tends to be the natural consequence of regional integration.

The second chapter of the second part, by Arturo O'Connell, examines some issues concerning the macroeconomic coordination in MERCOSUR. First, he shows that, even after almost a decade of a long process of integration and opening up of the MERCOSUR economies, their commercial dependence on each other was slim compared to that of the EU countries presently undergoing a process of monetary unification. Furthermore, liberalization of labour flows has hardly made any progress. Therefore, on the 'real' side, there is little that could be argued for macroeconomic coordination, let alone for a currency union among MERCOSUR countries. On the other hand, volatility in relative exchange rates has not necessarily had serious impacts on trade flows in the region. In fact, some studies on determinants of trade flows between Argentina and Brazil have shown a large response to changes in levels of activity in the destination country and a very small one to changes in exchange rates. O'Connell concludes that obstacles for MERCOSUR progress, therefore, have more to do with some microeconomic issues than with macroeconomic issues of relative exchange rates or coordination of fiscal and monetary policies. He suggests that for MERCOSUR countries to start on a new phase of sustainable development, it would be essential to overcome both their specific and more general weakness in their pattern of trade and external relations with the world at large. Only in this way could some degree of autonomy be pursued and achieved in terms of the policy aims of the member countries. So the question arises as to which policies would be instrumental in achieving those aims by overcoming what may be seen as obstacles to further development of MERCOSUR. According to O'Connell, the only way to gain more autonomy and be able to practise growth policies is through the development of competitiveness that could lead to a less vulnerable position, integrated in the world economy not only as a receiver of financial flows but as a dynamic exporter.

In the following chapter, Maria Luiza Silva, Joaquim Andrade and Hans-Michael Trautwein analyse some issues concerning the macroeconomy of MERCOSUR countries, in particular Brazil and Argentina. The coexistence of a fixed exchange rate regime within a currency board arrangement in Argentina and a more flexible exchange-rate system with strong sterilization policy in Brazil have challenged the sustainability of MERCOSUR regional integration. Even when both countries had fixed exchange rates in terms of the US dollar, domestic policy shocks tended to produce asymmetric adjustments, because Brazil largely neutralized the impact of intra-regional capital flows, whereas Argentina did not. In this constellation, trade integration would be favoured only by monetary expansion in Brazil or by fiscal expansion in Argentina; the difference in the monetary policy regimes may nevertheless have helped to buffer external shocks, as in the case of the Mexican crisis. However, the underlying asymmetry was exacerbated when Brazil switched to floating in 1999. Now even external shocks had clearly adverse effects on trade integration and on the synchronization of economic development in the region. Therefore, the differences in monetary policies have contributed to the asynchronization and asymmetries in the cyclical fluctuations of economic activity in Argentina and Brazil. Through the interaction between the different regimes, the impact of common external shocks to the region has been damp- ened in Brazil, whereas it has been amplified in Argentina. The monetary policy asymmetry is likely to have produced adverse long-run effects on the trade pattern and other target variables of economic integration in the MERCOSUR, thereby limiting the sustainability of regional integration. The authors conclude that the puzzle could be solved through a macroeconomic coordination arrangement. The lack of macroeconomic policy coordination in MERCOSUR has led to serious setbacks in the process of trade integration.

In the last chapter of the second part, Adriana Amado and Luiz Afonso Simoens analyse the perspective of monetary integration within MERCOSUR. The chapter is based on the Post-Keynesian tradition and points out some problems associated with monetary integration in economies that are struc- turally different. It also examines whether these differences are relevant to the MERCOSUR case. A theoretical framework is developed which emphasizes the point that to the extent that financial systems from integrated economies are structurally different, the 'logic of the market' tends to imply inequality, instead of convergence, in growth trajectories. It follows that financial systems with very different structures tend to reinforce the regional imbalances in terms of development. Consequently, it is necessary for regional blocs to adopt suitable institutional mechanisms to avoid the concentration and unstable tendencies of the market. The banking sectors of Argentina and Brazil are compared to show that: (i) in both countries the penetration of foreign banks has increased a great deal recently, but Argentina's is a more internationalized financial system than Brazil's; (ii) the indicators of financial deepening show that Brazil has a more developed financial system than Argentina; (iii) produc- tivity is higher in the banking sector in Argentina than in Brazil; and (iv) both countries have concentrated financial systems both in absolute and in regional terms. Two conclusions are derived from this comparison: first, in the case of financial integration, it would imply a flux of liquidity from Argentina to Brazil that would benefit the Brazilian banking sector; second, since both countries have concentrated financial systems, financial integration would also generate a tendency to exclude peripheral regions from the possible bene- fits of the process of integration. This issue could be aggravated by the fact that both countries have increasingly internationalized financial systems. Furthermore, since there are great differences in the degree of dollarization between Argentina and Brazil, the adoption of a single currency would be more problematic than otherwise. The chapter concludes that market forces cannot lead to monetary and financial integration. Instead, MERCOSUR's national governments must create institutions and financial mechanisms that favour a model of integration that stimulates social and economic growth.

In the first chapter of the third part, Rogério Studart analyses the effects of external financial integration between Latin American economies and mature economies. In the last two decades financial integration between these two groups has been rapid and significant. It has also been quite traumatic, because often followed by macroeconomic instability – exchange rate instability, poor growth performance and domestic financial crises. In the case of the MERCOSUR bloc, this associated macroeconomic instability has been a major obstacle to sustained trade integration among the four economies of the bloc. According to Studart, some analysts blame the volatility of capital flows for such perverse destabilizing effects, while others (mainly mainstream economists) centre their criticisms on the inconsistent domestic policies and lack of appropriate financial regulation and supervision in domestic Latin American economies. This chapter claims that this debate is missing the main issues behind such instability; these are (i) financial integration of Latin American economies in the 1990s has been the 'integration of uneven partners', that is, the integration of rapidly expanding capital-market-based systems with relatively stagnant bank-based systems; (ii) the consequences of such integration are destabilizing due to the volume, type and volatility of capital flows *vis-à-vis* the size and capacity of Latin American domestic financial markets to absorb such flows. The chapter concludes that the Latin American experience of the 1990s is not the first traumatic experience of financial opening and liberalization, and is unlikely to be the last. Two lessons can be drawn from this traumatic experience. First, if MERCOSUR or any other trade bloc in the region is to be sustainable in the future, one crucial target should be to avoid processes that lead to financial vulnerability of the economies. Second, and as a consequence of the first lesson, the deregulation of the capital and financial account should always be very gradual, respecting the structural asymmetries that exist between financial systems of developed and developing economies.

Finally, José Maria Fanelli and Daniel Heymann examine some causes of the collapse of the Argentine system of convertibility with a hard peg to the dollar and its consequences for the future of MERCOSUR. To begin with, they deal with the literature on monetary and exchange rate policies and show that even though there is no first best in the case of the choice of an exchange rate regime, in the context of open capital accounts credibly fixed rates may not be a viable long-run option for most countries, given the pervasive possibility of speculative attacks. This seems to be the case of the Argentine experience. It has been a feature of the Argentine economy that most assets of more than a few months' duration have been denominated in dollars. The diffusion of dollar contracting increased the costs of leaving convertibility. This character- istic, which derives from the uncertainties of agents with respect to monetary management, has implied that an expansion of longer-run credit carried with it the risk of currency mismatches if the exchange rate varied significantly. As a macroeconomic result economic downturns are associated with pressures on both financial and foreign exchange markets. There was thus a lock-in effect, derived mainly from the financial behaviour that had been induced under the monetary regime. Persistent fiscal deficits, especially after the 1994 reform of the social security system, caused a continuous increase in public debt. Further, when the economy went into recession, fiscal policies were burdened with a variety of demands, such as to contemplate increasing scepticism of creditors and claims for social spending, while tax revenues were falling. According to the authors, the 'internal drain' of deposits, combined with the 'external drain' of foreign reserves, the extreme difficulties of fiscal policies and the deepening recession acted jointly to generate explosive economic and social conditions in Argentina. They conclude that given the increased impor- tance of exports for Argentina, it may be argued that the possibility of restart- ing and developing integration may have a high cost. So, if Argentina manages to define a viable monetary–fiscal regime policy, and moves towards a normalization of the economy, a gradual process of macroeconomic coordina- tion with Brazil may appear a distinct possibility.

We wish to thank Edward Elgar and Dymphna Evans for their encouragement and close collaboration on this and, of course, on many other projects. As always we are hugely grateful to both of them and to their staff. We are also grateful to Fernando Ferrari for his help, both at Oxford University and later in Brazil, in the preparation of both the conference and this book. Most of the chapters included in this volume were presented to a conference at St Antony's College, University of Oxford, in June 2001, organized jointly by the Centre for Brazilian Studies and the Argentine Studies Programme, Latin American Centre. We are grateful to the Centre for Brazilian Studies, especially to its Director, Professor Leslie Bethell, and the staff of the Centre for their hospi- tality and encouragement to hold the conference. We also wish to thank Dr Celia Szusterman, director of the Argentine Studies Programme, for her work in the conception and organization of the conference.

NOTES

1. See, for instance, Chapter 3 of this volume.
2. See Chapters 5, 7 and 8 in this volume.

PART I

Lessons from the Euro and EMU for
MERCOSUR

1. Learning from, and about, EMU – a UK view[*]

John S. Flemming

This chapter has two themes, both more backward than forward looking. One is that of the conference, lessons of the European Monetary Union – EMU; the other is for me to review the suggestions I made to an audience in São Paulo almost exactly three years ago, focusing primarily on EMU.

I made the mistake then of suggesting that the euro would prove strong against the dollar and the yen. I was clearly wrong – but it is not clear that this carries any lesson for MERCOSUR.

I suggested that effective monetary union might come to MERCOSUR through spreading dollarization. That now look less likely. However, my suggestion that exchange rate or currency board linkage should not be to the US$ dollar alone but to a basket of dollar, yen and euro – possibly equally weighted – looks more promising. I believe that Argentina's problems owe more to the Brazilian devaluation than to the strength of the US dollar relative to the yen and the euro. But at least one of my forecasts was correct – that the ECB (European Central Bank) would give little weight in its deliberations to the external value of the euro, so that exchange rates between the three major currencies would be volatile in the sense of swinging widely if not wildly.

Turning now to the experience of EMU – what are its lessons? I do not think that the UK has learned very much. The process is, of course, not yet complete. It was only in January 2002 that European households would start to use euro notes and coins – and some did not expect that process to be entirely smooth. Although businesses have already been able to make price comparisons more easily with the assurance that they would not be disrupted by exchange rate movements, that seems to have had little perceptible effect on the intensity of competition. The Internet, of course, has some similar effects regardless of the exchange regime – and the domestication of the euro in 2002 may have given the process a further twist.

Some of my fears for EMU relate to the possibility that 'one-size-fits-all' monetary policy might leave some countries with untreated depression that could strengthen unhealthy political forces lurking in the wings in most European countries. This has not happened.

What has happened has been a boom, or set of booms, in a number of peripheral countries – such as Ireland and Portugal. This peripheral boom has its counterpart in a relatively sluggish core of France, and particularly Germany, but their relative weights in the ECB's aggregates are such that Germany's sluggishness is not ignored.

In the European case this is not a mere matter of chance. Before EMU, German economic and financial stability was rewarded with low real interest rates while its partners', particularly the Southern (Mediterranean) and Western (Atlantic) peripheral countries', currencies incurred a risk premium on top of any expected inflation differential reflected in their interest rates.

The effect of EMU has been virtually to eliminate the risk premium, while Germany's safe haven discount has also vanished. The shift in relative real rates has tended to shift investment from the core to the periphery, where it has generated boom conditions with inflationary effects – at least on the prices of non-tradable goods – thus further lowering perceived real interest rates relative to those in Germany.

Thus the process which is contributing to the convergence in living standards has some cumulatively divergent features too – as well as posing fiscal policy dilemmas for the booming peripheral economies, most notably Ireland.

I shall not pursue those further because I am not sure that MERCOSUR has a core and a periphery. In terms of market size, Brazil might be the core. Had its dollarization gone more smoothly, Argentina might have enjoyed the interest rate discount. But that has not happened, so I am not at all sure that there is a useful lesson here.

So far I have not addressed the question whether EMU had real-economy objectives and whether they have been achieved in ways that teach the lesson that monetary union works. To recapitulate, the argument was that the greater price transparency and the removal of exchange rate risk would enable competition and economies of scale to be traded off more favourably over the larger and more unified single European market.

This process was always going to take time, depending, as it did, on investment and corporate realignment and restructuring. While this might have proceeded, the full domestication of the euro is still in its early days. What we have seen is a certain amount of corporate takeover and restructuring activity. Some of this, such as Vodaphone's takeover of Mannesmann, has been cross-border and part of a global industrial development. But many others, such as Allianz–Dresdner, are largely within one country – and we have seen EdF use its French electricity monopoly to take controversial stakes in its neighbours' privatized electricity industries.

Despite the ten-year-old single market and the two-year-old euro the European market in corporate control is far from being free and unified. Germany has just blocked a directive on European takeovers. Mergers that create national champions do little to take advantage of any potential improvement in the scale/competition trade-off.

Thus so far it is hard to identify the realization of the real-economy gains that had been hoped for. Another test is whether the euro is popular. On this we have some mixed messages. Greece felt that qualifying for membership enhanced its self-respect. The Danish people felt no such need and, in a referendum, rejected the advice of the whole of its political industrial élite to join. In Germany we are told that people's enthusiasm for giving up the Deutschmark showed no sign of growing as 'Eday' neared. For several years now popular support there for EMU has waned as people's estimate of the probability and proximity of its occurrence has waxed.

Finally, of course, one might ask what lessons the UK has learned from its close vantage point and its self-imposed exclusion. The main lessons drawn are rather mixed – not to say inconsistent.

On the one hand the tabloid press has enjoyed some *schadenfreude* at the weakness of the euro. On the other hand the industrial lobby has been pressing for early entry on the curious grounds that had the UK joined at the start it would not have suffered the consequences of a 20 per cent loss of competitiveness *vis-à-vis* the Continent. If the UK is to join, that loss will have to be made good in some way that does not stimulate inflation or prompt the MPC (Monetary Policy Committee) to discredit the idea by raising interest rates sharply. It is surprising how, until very recently, the overvaluation of the pound has been absorbed by UK industry.

Let me close by noting that the UK electorate is believed at this point to be 70 per cent against entry, while Prime Minister Blair believes that he has unstated arguments and procedures up his sleeve which will reduce that to 49 per cent or less within three years.

For now, at least, the UK people's advice to those contemplating monetary union would appear to be that of Mr Punch to those contemplating matrimony – don't. That advice has, of course, rarely been heeded and in several such cases, as Dr Johnson observed, hope has triumphed over experience – and that may apply to the hopes of MERCOSUR in the light of the European experience.

NOTE

* This chapter was prepared specially for the workshop 'Towards Macroeconomic Convergence in MERCOSUR? Lessons from the European Monetary Union', held at St Antony's College, University of Oxford, 12 June 2001.

2. The euro and the EMU: lessons for MERCOSUR*

Philip Arestis, Fernando Ferrari-Filho, Luiz Fernando de Paula and Malcolm Sawyer

1. INTRODUCTION

In 1991, the Asunción Treaty, signed by Argentina, Brazil, Paraguay and Uruguay, created the Common Market of the South (hereafter MERCOSUR). At that time, MERCOSUR was created to be *only* a customs union that came into effect on 1 January 1995. The MERCOSUR experience has been characterized by economic turbulences: in January 1999, the Brazilian currency, the real, was devaluated and, as a result, it brought some spillover effects in the MERCOSUR area; recently, more specifically, at the end of 2001 and beginning of 2002, the economic, political and institutional crises in Argentina, characterized by the collapse of the Convertibility Plan[1] – that is to say, the devaluation of Argentine currency – the default of Argentine foreign debt and tensions among governments and socioeconomic actors,[2] have caused further macroeconomic instability to the MERCOSUR countries. This raises the question of whether a monetary union in this area is the way forward. In 1998 the annual regional summit of MERCOSUR actually indicated the possibility of creating a single currency. In December 2000, macroeconomic convergence criteria that included inflation rates, fiscal deficits, public sector debt and balance of payments, were suggested as a way forward.[3] Academic debate in South America favours a MERCOSUR monetary union based on the European Economic and Monetary Union (EMU), and inspired by the theory of optimal currency area (OCA): Edwards, 1998; Rigolon and Giambiagi, 1999; Giambiagi, 1999, provide a representative sample.

The EMU was founded in January 1999 along with the European Central Bank (ECB), and the launch of the single currency (euro). The euro was established for financial transactions with the exchange rates between those national currencies that will eventually be absorbed by the euro, and fixed (to six significant figures). The euro will replace the component national currencies for all transactions in the first two months of 2002 (the precise dates and arrangements varying between countries). The value of the euro has declined through most of the period of its existence from an initial value *vis-à-vis* the dollar of $1.18 to parity with the dollar in December 1999, an all-time low in November 2000 of $0.82, and to around $0.87 at the time of revising this chapter, February 2002. We have explored the explanations for that decline elsewhere (Arestis et al., 2002).

The EMU constitutes a change in the economic, social and political spheres of Europe. Inevitably, it has been the subject of intense debate. The single currency has served to concentrate many diverse aspects of the debate around one question: is the euro in the interests of Europe? And for the purposes of this chapter: is the euro experiment a good example for MERCOSUR to adopt? We argue that the economic impact of the euro, and its accompanying monetary institutions, is likely to be deflationary and destabilizing. We do not, however, argue that the project of a single European currency is inherently flawed, but rather that the institutional and policy arrangements within which it is embedded are flawed. On the contrary, we have proposed elsewhere (Arestis, McCauley and Sawyer, 2001) a Keynesian alternative to the economic policies and institutions that currently surround the euro. In this way, we argue that the broad question is not whether to be 'for' or 'against' the euro *per se*, but to get the 'right' institutional framework and policy for the achievement of high employment levels throughout the Union. Lessons based on the euro and the EMU approach will be derived for MERCOSUR in this chapter.

We proceed in section 2 to examine the institutional structure of the euro experiment before we turn our attention to its theoretical underpinnings. Sections 3 and 4 discuss the problematic nature of both the institutional arrangements and the theoretical framework, respectively, upon which they are based. We then concentrate on the lessons for MERCOSUR that may be drawn from the EMU experience. The realities of the MERCOSUR proposed arrangements are the focus of section 6. A final section summarizes the argument and concludes.

2. INSTITUTIONAL UNDERPINNINGS

The euro was adopted in January 1999, with the member currencies locked together from that point, and with the intention that the euro be used as the sole currency in the participating countries from early 2002. Criteria were set down under the Maastricht Treaty that were supposed to be met by those seeking to join the euro (see Arestis, Brown and Sawyer, 2001). The convergence criteria were in nominal terms, with no mention of real convergence or even of business cycle convergence. They included a budget deficit and a government debt criterion designed to establish 'fiscal responsibility' in the eyes of the financial markets and had no underlying rationale. The independence of the ECB, and that of national central banks, was also part of the list of these criteria. In terms of countries meeting the criteria, it must be said that with the exception of the inflation rate and the interest rate, they were not met as comfortably as might have appeared initially. In fact a great deal of 'fudging' took place, and that may have added to the subsequent weakness of the euro. In the event, 11 countries out of the 15 member countries of the EU were deemed to have met both these criteria and joined the EMU (Greece was not included initially, but in January 2001 was deemed to have met the criteria and is now a member of the EMU).

The institutional arrangements accompanying the euro involve the creation of an 'independent' (of political control) European System of Central Banks (ESCB) with its operating arm, the ECB and the national central banks, given the sole policy objective of price stability, defined as a year-on-year increase in the Harmonized Index of Consumer Prices (HICP) for the euro area of below 2 per cent over the medium term. The dominant feature of the ECB's institutional structure is the complete separation between the monetary authorities (in the form of the Central Bank) and the fiscal authorities (in the shape of the national governments comprising the EMU), where the latter are constrained to keep their budget deficit below 3 per cent according to the Stability and Growth Pact, noting that this implies a budget position in balance or slight surplus over the course of the business cycle. It follows that there can be little coordination of monetary and fiscal policy. The euro system is perhaps unique in having a 'high-level' monetary authority (the ECB) and in effect no 'high-level' fiscal authority, with fiscal policy residing at the national level (albeit constrained by the Stability and Growth Pact). There cannot be any substantive coordination of monetary and fiscal policies in these circumstances, and there is a sense in which the monetary authority has the last word in that interest rates are set frequently and can be adjusted to seek to offset any fiscal policy. It is also the case that the independence of the ECB and the national central banks places heavy constraints on any coordination of fiscal and monetary policy. For example, 'neither the ECB, nor a national central bank, nor any member of their decision making bodies shall seek or take instructions from Community institutions or bodies, from any government of a Member States or from any other body' (Article 7 of *The Statute of the European System of Central Banks and of the European Central Bank*). Any strict interpretation of this edict would rule out any attempt at coordination of monetary and fiscal policies. Indeed, the primacy of monetary policy over fiscal policy is guaranteed because of the institutional structure and rules of the ESCB.

The Stability and Growth Pact, which accompanied the introduction of a single currency, governs the economic policies of the member countries which have joined the single currency and strongly constrains the policies of those who aspire to join. It is an important dimension of the institutional framework of the EMU, and as such we need to discuss it at some length.

Stability and Growth Pact

The Stability and Growth Pact, alongside the Maastricht Treaty, creates four rules for economic policy: the independence of the ECB from political influence; the introduction of the 'no bail-out of national government deficits' rule; the prohibition of monetary financing of government deficits; and avoidance by member states of 'excessive' deficits (defined as more than 3 per cent of GDP).

A government which aims to avoid an 'excessive' budget deficit of more than 3 per cent of GDP would have to ensure that the 3 per cent limit is not breached during economic slowdown; and hence that the average deficit during the course of the business cycle would have to be much lower than 3 per cent. A country's budgetary data become available for the Commission to scrutinize on 1 March each year, when the stability programmes are submitted. Each programme contains information about the paths of the ratios of budget deficit to GDP and national debt to GDP. The Council (ECOFIN) examines the stability reports and delivers an opinion on a recommendation by the Commission (within two months of the reports' submission). If the stability programme reveals that a country is diverging significantly from its medium-term budgetary objective, then the council recommends that the stability programme be strengthened. If the situation persists, then the member state has been judged to have breached the reference values. The Pact details 'escape' clauses which allow a member state that has an excessive deficit to avoid sanction. If there is an economic downturn and output has fallen by more than 2 per cent, then the member state escapes sanction automatically, but the deficit should be corrected once the recession has finished. If output falls between 0.75 and 2 per cent, then the Council can use discretion when making a decision on an 'excessive' deficit; other factors are taken into account such as the abruptness of the downturn, the accumulated loss of output relative to past trends and whether the government deficit exceeds government investment expenditure.

If a country is found to have breached the reference values, it has four months to introduce the corrective measures suggested by the Council. If the country follows the Council's recommendations, then the 'excessive' deficit can continue, but the budget deficit must be corrected within a year following its identification. A country which chooses not to introduce corrective measures is subject to a range of sanctions (Article 104c(11)), at least one or more of which must be imposed, including one in the form of a non-interest-bearing deposit lodged by the national government. In this instance, it falls upon EMU members, excluding the member country under consideration, to reach a decision on sanctions. The non-interest-bearing deposit consists of a fixed component (0.2 per cent of GDP), and a variable component (one-tenth of the difference between the deficit ratio and the 3 per cent reference value). If the budget deficit is not corrected within two years, the deposit is forfeited and becomes a fine, whereas if the deficit is corrected within two years the deposit is returned and the penalty becomes the foregone interest.

This system of financial penalties for breaches of the budget deficit criterion implies that deflationary fiscal policies continue, and indeed intensify, as those countries which just met the 3 per cent requirement in conditions of cyclical upswing have to tighten the fiscal stance to meet the 3 per cent requirement especially in times of cyclical downswing. It was indicated above that a clause was inserted into the Stability and Growth Pact which allows a country to have a larger deficit in the face of recession. However, even this formal recognition that automatic stabilizers and active fiscal policy could be hampered may not be sufficient to prevent the Stability and Growth Pact operating to exacerbate recessions.

The overall conclusion of the discussion in this section is that a number of problems can be identified in view of the EMU and the euro institutional arrangements. For the purposes of our study two of these can be highlighted. The first is that fiscal policy is in effect absent (other than, of course, directives to member states emanating from the Stability and Growth Pact); monetary policy is given priority over fiscal policy, and coordination of fiscal and monetary policies is prohibited. At both national and EU level, the use of fiscal policy is heavily constrained by the Stability and Growth Pact. The second is that the institutional set-up produces a certain bias for deflationary tendencies. The experience since 1999 in terms of the ECB monetary policy performance, especially the reluctance of the ECB to reduce interest rates (more recently such reduction has taken place only after enormous pressure by the US and other national governments, the IMF and World Bank, and other international fora), clearly testifies to the bias just mentioned. Further examples may be noted: the recent condemnation of Ireland for cutting taxes and raising public expenditure when output was above trend; criticisms of the UK, even though outside the eurozone, for proposing public expenditure increases above the trend rate of growth of output point to a general deflationary bias in the operation of the Stability and Growth Pact. It also means that governments are put under pressure to raise taxes and/or cut government spending under recessionary circumstances, which exacerbates the downturn. This is illustrated by the recent (April 2001) recommendation to the British government (who are not formally governed by the Stability and Growth Pact) that in the event of a downturn in 2002, public expenditure should be reduced (below planned levels) to maintain the public expenditure to GDP ratio. It thus follows that macroeconomic policy at the EMU level has been designed to operate in a restrictive manner. The ECB pursues extremely cautionary rules, presumably in its attempt to gain 'credibility' in the financial markets at the cost of any other objectives. A serious implication at this juncture is that with the US slowdown, which threatens to produce a world recession, EMU policy could potentially help to avoid it. The ECB policy stance at the moment does not appear to be geared to this objective.

3. THEORETICAL UNDERPINNINGS

The theoretical underpinnings of the EMU institutional structure appear to be based on what we have elsewhere termed new monetarism (Arestis and Sawyer, 1998). The essential features of new monetarism are:

1. Politicians in particular, and the democratic process in general, cannot be trusted with economic policy formulation, with a tendency to make decisions which have stimulating short-term effects (reducing unemployment) but which are detrimental in the longer term (notably a rise in inflation). In contrast, experts in the form of central bankers are not subject to political pressures and can thus take a longer-term perspective. The logic underpinning this reasoning mirrors that found in the rules versus discretion debate. Policy makers' scope for using discretion should be curtailed and the possibility of negative spillovers from irresponsible fiscal policy must be reduced within the euro system. Consequently, fiscal policy is permanently constrained by the Stability and Growth Pact and monetary policy is removed from national and political authorities and placed with the ECB.
2. Inflation is a monetary phenomenon and can be controlled through monetary policy. Although money supply is difficult to control directly, it is none the less useful as a reference magnitude. The ECB can set the key interest rate to influence monetary conditions, which in turn influence the future rate of inflation.
3. A 'two-pillar' monetary strategy is actually pursued. This may be briefly summarized: the 'first pillar' is a commitment to analyse monetary developments for the information they contain about future price developments. This is the quantitative reference value for monetary growth (4.5 per cent of M3) referred to in the text. The 'second pillar' is a broadly based assessment of the outlook of price developments and the risks to price stability. This broad range of indicators includes the euro exchange

rate, labour market indicators (such as wages and unit labour costs), fiscal policy indicators, financial market indicators (such as asset prices), and so on.

4. The level of unemployment fluctuates around a supply-side determined equilibrium rate of unemployment, generally labelled the NAIRU (non-accelerating inflation rate of unemployment). The level of the NAIRU may be favourably affected by a 'flexible' labour market, but is unaffected by the level of aggregate demand or by productive capacity.

5. Fiscal policy is impotent in terms of its impact on real variables and as such it should be subordinate to monetary policy in controlling inflation. It is recognized, though, that the government budget position will fluctuate during the course of the business cycle but in the context of an essentially passive fiscal policy. The main feature of the Stability and Growth Pact is a requirement that the national budget deficit does not exceed 3 per cent of GDP, and failure to meet that requirement could lead to a series of fines depending on the degree to which the deficit exceeds 3 per cent (as further discussed below). Non-euro members are also required to exercise similar fiscal control through convergence programmes, though they are not subject to excessive deficit penalties.

The economic policy implications that lie behind this type of analysis are that macroeconomic demand conditions, including monetary and fiscal policies, cannot affect the (equilibrium) level of unemployment of labour, and in more general terms the level of economic activity. The level of unemployment and of economic activity is viewed as solely a supply-side phenomenon. An important problematic aspect of this policy framework is the symmetry or otherwise of shocks. Given the one-instrument-only nature of monetary policy within the euro system, the extent of asymmetrical shocks becomes paramount. If shocks are indeed asymmetrical, the one-policy framework cannot tackle effectively even the one-target objective of price stability. From the perspective of the business cycle, it could be argued that Ireland, with output above trend to the extent of over 2.5 per cent of GDP, and Italy, with output below trend to the extent of 2.5 per cent of GDP, require quite different macroeconomic policies. The optimists would tend to believe that the introduction of the euro and the continuing effects of the single market would lead to further integration between the national economies. This integration could then be reflected in some convergence between national business cycles and a reduction in the extent of asymmetric shocks (that is, shocks that affect some economies but not others). If there were full integration between the national economies, then a unified economic policy would be appropriate, though we would argue that a single policy instrument such as interest rates is not sufficient to achieve multiple objectives.

4.   POLITICAL UNION AND/OR ECONOMIC CONVERGENCE?

One might have expected that the formation of the EMU, encompassing 12 politically independent countries each with their own currencies before the Union, would be much influenced by economic convergence and political union considerations. It is the purpose of this section to demonstrate that neither of these considerations has been influential in creating and shaping the EMU and the euro.

Political Union

Table 2.1 divides monetary unions into a number of categories. The first category includes those unions that survive with political union as well. Political union ensures the success of the monetary union. The examples referred to in Table 2.1 are obvious enough. The second category includes unions of small countries that have survived without political union. These unions have survived because of economic convergence, with varying degrees of success. The third category is where the survival of the union depends crucially on the political system. As soon as the political bond disappears, so does the monetary union. The fourth category is an obvious one: once economic links collapse, the union disappears. The fifth category contains temporary monetary unions. They survive for some time without political union but eventually collapse when they are subjected to severe shocks (in the example of Table 2.1, the suspension of the gold standard at the beginning of World War I that led to volatility in real exchange rates, and the inflationary pressures following the cessation of hostilities, were the main causes). A sixth category represents currency pegs and other systems. This is an example that demonstrates the importance of flexibility, particularly pertinent when currency systems attempt to bind together economies whose cycles and structures are significantly different.

There are two important lessons that can be derived from this short excursion into the history of monetary unions. The first is that political union appears to be an extremely important prerequisite for a monetary union to survive. Monetary unions last for some time but eventually they must become a political union to survive. The second is that economic convergence when political union is not present is paramount for the survival of a monetary union of small independent states.

A belief that a market economy will function effectively without government intervention and redistribution would obviate any need for economic policies within the eurozone. The eurozone begins with considerable economic disparities. The vies that either they will be eliminated through a

Table 2.1   Monetary unions

Still surviving but with political union	
British monetary union between England and Scotland	From 1707
Italian monetary union	From 1861
US Federal Reserve system	From 1913
German unification	From 1990
Still surviving without political union	
Belgium–Luxembourg union	From 1923
West and Central African CFA Franc Zone[a]	From 1948
Eastern Caribbean Currency Union[b]	From 1983
Failed once political system collapsed	
Roman monetary union[c]	286–301
German monetary union	1857–1918
The Soviet system	1917–93
Yugoslavia	1919–92
Czechoslovak Republic	1919–94
Failed once economic links collapsed	
British monetary union between England and Ireland	1926–79
Temporary monetary unions	
Latin monetary union[d]	1865–1926
Scandinavian currency union[e]	1873–1921
Other currency pegs	
Gold standard	1870–1931/36
Bretton Woods	1944–73
ERM	From 1979
Asian currency crisis	1997

Notes:

[a] CFA: Common Franc Area (Benin, Burkina Faso, Cameroon, Central African Republic, Chad, Congo, Equatorial Guinea, Gabon, Ivory Coast, Mali, Niger, Senegal and Togo); after 1 January 1999 the peg is linked to the euro.

[b] This Union includes: Anguilla, Antigua and Barbuda, Commonwealth of Dominica, Grenada, Montserrat, St Kitts and Nevis, St Lucia, St Vincent and The Grenadines.

[c] Emperor Diocletian reforms Roman coinage, thereby creating the first single currency union.

[d] This Union included: Fance, Belgium, Italy and Switzerland; Greece and Bulgaria joined in 1867. The link changed from silver to gold in 1878.

[e] This Union was established between Denmark and Sweden in May 1873 (both almost joined the Latin Union but eventually did not because of the Franco-Prussian War of 1870–71). Norway joined in October 1875.

Sources: Adapted from *The Financial Times* (23 March 1998) and Pentecost (1999).

process of market competition or that such disparities are politically sustainable would lead to the conclusion that there is little requirement for an effective political union. In effective political union we would include significant EU-level taxation, social security and public expenditure programmes. We leave open the question as to whether that would entail a formal political union within a federal state. We would argue that the effective operation of a market economy involves government intervention of that form. A common social security system would enhance labour mobility as well as involve elements of redistribution. A substantive fiscal policy would likewise aid economic integration but would involve significant fiscal transfers between regions and between countries.

The present arrangements governing the euro do not involve mechanisms for the reduction of the disparities of unemployment and GDP per head. The disparities of unemployment inevitably undermine the achievement of high levels of employment across the eurozone. While some regions are experiencing low unemployment and high rates of capacity utilization, others remain with high unemployment. Inflation pressures, actual or perceived, in the low-unemployment regions will lead high interest rates and attempts to slow down the eurozone economy. A monetary union involves the imposition of a common currency across a number of nations through the requirement that the common currency be the only legal tender within the nations involved. In that trivial sense, a monetary union involves a degree of political agreement, if not political union. There is also the obvious requirement for a central bank for the monetary union, and in an era of dominance of monetary policy over fiscal policy, that central bank becomes the effective macroeconomic policy maker. Any requirements for an effective fiscal policy across the monetary union would be redistributive across time and space, pointing in the direction of the emergence of a fiscal authority at the level of the monetary union. Further requirements, such as measures to enhance trade or for a common social security system to enhance labour mobility, again point in the direction of policies being exercised at the level of the monetary union. It might be said that such policies could be introduced through the construction of institutions at the level of the monetary union without formal political union. But in a number of respects, if there were fiscal policy, social security policy and so on at the level of the monetary union, this would come close to being a political union. We would suggest, though, that a monetary union requires considerable central government to operate fiscal and social security policies across the eurozone.

Economic Convergence

The second conclusion reached from our discussion of Table 2.1 is that of economic convergence. Although this conclusion concerns small states, the argument can easily be generalized. It might be expected that any monetary union encompassing a number of politically independent countries, each with their own currencies before the union, would be much influenced by optimal currency area (OCA) considerations. We suggest, though, that OCA considerations had virtually no impact on the decision to introduce a single European currency nor on the conditions governing which countries were to be members. It ought to be noted, though, that the single currency was preceded by the Single European Act, which created a single market involving more than just free trade in that it sought to bring in common standards for goods and services, reduction of 'invisible' trade barriers, and mobility (at least legally) of labour and capital. There were also, of course, the Maastricht criteria as explored above, but they related to convergence in nominal variables at a particular point in time, and made no reference to convergence in real variables (whether in terms of levels such as GDP per head or rates of change and position within the business cycle). Nor was there any reference to what could be termed structural convergence in terms of institutional and organizational arrangement.

The relevant literature suggests three conditions for an 'optimal currency area' (Mundell, 1961; see also McKinnon, 1963, and Kenen, 1969): (a) factor mobility and openness of markets; (b) relative price flexibility; and (c) fiscal transfers within the monetary union. It would be desirable for a single currency to be used in an economic area within which there is openness of goods markets and mobility of factors of production (labour, capital), as the mobility of factors is seen as one way in which adjustment is made to differences in economic performance. Further, member economies should share similar inflationary tendencies since a common currency imposes a common inflation rate. The Single European Act of 1986 and the implementation of the single European market by the end of 1992 were steps in seeking to ensure the mobility of goods and services and of capital within the European Union. But it is well known that effective labour mobility with the EU remains low, especially by comparison with the USA, despite the large differences in real wages and unemployment rates across the EU. Price flexibility (in terms of relative prices across countries) remains low. The differences in labour market institutions, notably over wage determination, mean that there are different inflationary tendencies and different responses to economic shocks. The convergence criteria ensured a convergence of inflation rates, which is not the same as convergence of inflationary mechanisms and tendencies. Indeed, similar rates of inflation across the eurozone countries in 1998 (the relevant year for the application of the convergence criteria) were accompanied by widely differing rates of unemployment, from around 4 per cent in the case of Austria and the Netherlands to 17 per cent in the case of Spain (and the difference in unemployment between regions was much more marked, from 3 per cent in the Oberösterreich region of Austria to 32 per cent in the Andalucía region of Spain and nearly 37 per cent in Réunion, France (these figures refer to 1997). The calculated output gap, as a sign of the stage of the business cycle, varied (according to the OECD measure) from over +2 per cent in Ireland to –2 per cent in Italy (and there was a slight widening of the differences in 1999). Fiscal transfers are hardly in evidence and there is no possibility of the EU budget operating as a stabiliser. There is currently no mechanism for the operation of an EU level fiscal policy that could have stabilising effects (as an automatic stabilizer) over time nor which has any significant redistributive element across economic regions.

The optimists would tend to believe that the continuing effects of the single European market and the introduction of the euro will lead to further integration between the national economies. This integration could then be reflected in some convergence between national business cycles and (perhaps) some reduction in the extent of asymmetric shocks that affect some countries but not others. There could, in the fullness of time, be increased mobility of labour. But there seems little prospect of EU-wide measures such as a common social security policy which would enhance the mobility of labour. In any case, we have demonstrated elsewhere (Arestis et al., 2002) that since the introduction of the euro in January 1999, there is no evidence that economic convergence has taken place or is in sight of materializing.

This brief discussion indicates to us that OCA considerations appear to have played little role in the formation of the eurozone. Further, if the OCA literature is correct, then the eurozone would appear not to be an optimal currency area. Some of the departures of the eurozone from an OCA arise from policy decisions (notably the absence of an EU fiscal policy), whereas others (notably lack of labour mobility) are more deeply embedded, and some attempts have been made to address them (for example development of transferability of qualifications between countries). But to say that the eurozone is not optimal is not the same as saying that the eurozone is not better than the continuation of national currencies. However, we would argue that it is still the case that the criteria proposed by the OCA literature have some relevance in judging whether the introduction of the euro is an improvement. The point remains that the OCA literature has been ignored.

5. LESSONS FOR MERCOSUR

In this chapter we have touched upon the most important problems arising from the creation of the EMU. The implications of these for moves towards some form of monetary union among the MERCOSUR countries may now be summarized.

Our discussion of the OCA literature enables us to conclude that decisions on the EMU have not accounted for the concerns of that literature. In the formation of the eurozone there seems little possibility of significant labour mobility or fiscal policy being used in this way. We see this as a considerable weakness in the formation of EMU, and would argue that any eventual MERCOSUR monetary union should pay attention to these issues. A related lesson is the question of whether a sustainable monetary union requires a considerable degree of political integration, and eventually a political union. We have attempted to supply an answer based merely on the history of monetary unions. Our answer on this basis is positive. We would also suggest that in the absence of a political union, a minimum of a pan-union fiscal policy and a social security system operating at the level of the monetary union is desperately required. The diversity of economic performance, institutional arrangements and beliefs about economic policy and the operation of market economies are all further difficulties in the construction of a monetary union.

The introduction of a monetary union obviously creates a union-level monetary policy. It is widely recognized that monetary policy imposes a single policy applying across a diverse set of economic regions. A particular monetary policy may be appropriate for the position of some economies but not for others, given their position in the business cycle and the responsiveness of their economies to monetary policy. Moreover, such a policy is more likely to favour the politically strongest (even when operated by an 'independent' central bank). Further, monetary policy is constructed to deal with demand-induced inflation, with interest rates raised (lowered) in response to inflation (actual or expected) above (below) the target rate, though we would doubt the effectiveness of monetary policy to significantly influence aggregate demand. But monetary policy cannot deal with other forms of inflation (for example cost push inflation) nor with situations in which there is high (or rising) inflation combined with low (or falling) levels of economic activity. The monetary union requires a further set of policy instruments, including fiscal policy.

In the section that follows, we discuss the degree of severity of the 'lessons' just identified for MERCOSUR. We take the view that the 'lessons' in terms of a union-level monetary policy and that of a political union are serious problemss that would have to be resolved before any move towards a monetary union of MERCOSUR. This is actually reminiscent of the debates over financial liberalization in terms of the concerns expressed over the sequencing of institutional and policy changes. It could be argued that a similar concern should arise with monetary union, namely, whether monetary union should precede economic and political integration or come after considerable integration. Unlike the current advocates of the formation of the European single currency, we are of the opinion that monetary union should come after other economic and social integration has materialized. This is probably the most important question arising from the European experience that we see as of particular relevance for monetary union and dollarization in the case of MERCOSUR. As for the realities relating to the OCA possibility, we refer to the experience of the MERCOSUR countries since 1991 and examine the extent to which convergence has been taking place. This is precisely the aim of the section that follows.

6.   THE REALITIES OF MERCOSUR

We begin with the evidence on trade integration among the countries of MERCOSUR. Although intra-regional trade among the MERCOSUR countries increased more than three times between 1991 and 2000, these countries still export, on average, less than 2.0 per cent of GDP.[4] Even though the trade in the region increased in the 1990s, its importance compared to GDP is still very low. Intra-MERCOSUR trade is more important, however, for Uruguay and Argentina than for Brazil and Paraguay (see Table 2.2). So the degree of openness of the MERCOSUR countries is still low, as well as the size of the economies involved in trade since their relative share in the world economy is only around 4 per cent. In particular, Brazil and Argentina, in spite of the recent increase in intra-regional trade, are still very closed economies in terms of international trade. Paraguay and Uruguay are more open economies, but they clearly play a very small economic role in MERCOSUR.

Turning to capital mobility, the recent financial liberalization in the MERCOSUR area has intensified concentration in the financial markets instead of promoting competition in the national banking systems. The available evidence shows that financial liberalization in the 1990s has stimulated the concentration process in the financial and banking system (especially in Brazil; see, for example, Paula, 1998; Paula et al., 1999; Meirelles, 1999). Furthermore, the institutional arrangements throughout MERCOSUR concerning the mobility of capital are quite asymmetric. Uruguay has adopted a sort of crawling peg system since the beginning of the 1990s, using a band so that the currency can float with explicit linkage to price stabilization objectives. Paraguay has recently adopted a flexible exchange rate system, and saw its exchange rate being devalued at the same time. Argentina adopted a classical currency board system since the beginning of the 1990s, pegging the peso to the dollar on a one-to-one basis, with clear stabilization objectives. Recently, as we have already noted, the Argentine currency was devalued and the central bank began to operate a floating exchange rate regime. Brazil has operated a floating exchange rate regime since the beginning of 1999, following a period of operating a crawling peg system. There is also the important consideration that since capital flows depend on the degree of financial development, and in

Table 2.2　Macroeconomic data – MERCOSUR

	GDP (% annual growth)[a]				Unemployment rate[b]				Foreign debt/	
Year	Argentina	Brazil	Paraguay	Uruguay	Argentina	Brazil	Paraguay	Uruguay	Argentina	Brazil
1991	10.6	1.0	2.5	3.5	6.5	4.8	5.1	8.9	32.3	30.4
1992	9.6	–0.5	1.8	7.9	7.0	5.8	5.3	9.0	27.4	34.8
1993	5.7	4.9	4.1	2.7	9.6	5.4	5.1	8.3	30.5	33.1
1994	5.8	5.9	3.1	7.3	11.5	5.1	4.4	9.2	33.3	27.1
1995	–2.8	4.2	4.7	–1.4	17.5	4.6	5.3	10.3	38.2	22.6
1996	5.5	2.7	1.3	5.6	17.2	5.4	8.2	11.9	40.3	23.2
1997	8.1	3.3	2.6	4.9	14.9	5.7	7.1	11.5	42.6	24.8
1998	3.9	0.2	–0.4	4.6	12.9	7.6	6.6	10.1	47.0	30.7
1999	–3.4	0.9	1.4	–3.2	14.3	7.6	9.4	11.3	51.1	45.6
2000	0.0	4.0	4.0	–1.0	15.1	7.5	10.7	13.4	51.3	39.2

Notes:

[a] Percentages based on values at 1995 prices.

[b] Only urban unemployment; unemployment rate is according to international rules (for more details see *Statistical Yearbook for Latin America*, 2000: www.eclac.cl/estadisticas/)

[c] Balance at the end of year (includes the public and private sector external debt, and also IMF loans).

view of the low degree of financial deepening in the MERCOSUR countries, capital inflows are expected to be low (see Ferrari-Filho, 2002).

Labour mobility is relatively low within the MERCOSUR area. In particular, the mobility of labour between the two bigger countries, Brazil and Argentina, has been historically very low, and this is currently still very much in evidence. In practice, it is not difficult to demonstrate why labour mobility is relatively low, and two reasons suggest themselves: there are different technical and professional qualifications among the workers of the MERCOSUR countries, and labour markets in the area are regulated.

The figures cited in Tables 2.2 and 2.3 show that for the period 1991 to 2000 it is difficult to argue in favour of convergence. We comment on Table 2.2 and leave for later the discussion relating to Table 2.3. Table 2.2 cites data for the period 1991–2000 and for a number of macroeconomic variables: GDP growth rates, unemployment rates, foreign debt as a percentage of GDP, intra-MERCOSUR exports as a percentage of the aggregate of intra-MERCOSUR exports, and nominal interest rates. Taking GDP growth and unemployment rates together, Argentina and Uruguay have low growth rates (negative or zero) and high and rising unemployment rates. By contrast, Brazil and Paraguay enjoy positive and, in the year 2000, healthy growth rates, and relatively low unemployment rates (in the case of Brazil this rate falls slightly in 2000). The evolution of these variables during the 1990s shows a disparity between Argentina and Uruguay on the one hand, and Brazil and Paraguay on

GDP[c]		MERCOSUR exports/total exports[d]				Nominal interest rates[e]			
Paraguay	Uruguay	Argentina	Brazil	Paraguay	Uruguay	Argentina	Brazil	Paraguay	Uruguay
26.2	28.4	16.7	7.3	17.8	31.2	61.7	536.9	34.9	75.2
19.4	26.3	18.5	11.5	10.0	27.8	16.8	1549.2	28.0	54.5
18.2	23.9	28.0	14.0	10.5	40.4	11.3	3060.0	30.1	39.4
16.2	24.3	30.0	13.6	11.9	46.9	8.1	1153.8	35.5	37.0
16.0	22.9	32.1	13.1	11.6	46.6	11.9	53.1	33.9	38.2
14.9	22.8	32.9	15.3	15.5	44.9	7.4	27.4	31.9	28.1
15.4	21.9	36.0	17.0	20.1	46.5	7.0	24.8	27.8	19.6
18.8	23.1	35.6	17.4	18.5	53.0	7.6	24.8	30.5	15.1
27.2	24.5	30.0	14.2	18.3	43.4	8.1	25.6	30.2	14.2
33.8	27.2	31.9	14.0	17.2	43.5	8.0	17.4	16.4	8.1

[d] This ratio is each country's exports to the rest of MERCOSUR (i.e. intra-MERCOSUR exports) as a percentage of the aggregate of these exports (total exports).

[e] Central bank's basic interest rate.

Source: CEPAL/ECLAC (2001) (www.cepal.org), Mercosul (2001) (www.mercosul.org) and Inter-American Development Bank (2001) (www.jadb.org).

the other, both in terms of GDP growth and rate of unemployment. MERCO-SUR economies also exhibit a high degree of volatility in terms of these variables, indicating that they are subject to substantial shocks. This seems to suggest that there are asymmetric cyclical conditions in the economies of the region, and the magnitude of the co-movement of their business cycles is small, a suggestion that is supported by Valdovinos (2000) for a longer period.[5]

High foreign debt to GDP ratios are reported for all countries, but these are nearly twice as high in the case of Argentina and Brazil. Intra-MERCOSUR exports as a percentage of total exports have been decreasing since 1997. Nominal interest rates present an interesting picture. They tend to fall over the period, but they are extremely high in Brazil over the period 1991–94, with a substantial drop in 1995 following the sharp decrease in inflation with the introduction of a price stabilization programme (known as the Real Plan). By 1998, though, and following the Russian crisis, interest rates rise in Argentina, Brazil and Paraguay (only to fall again in 1999 in Brazil and Paraguay), but continue to fall in Uruguay. An interesting pattern emerges. Argentina is a low-interest-rate country, while Brazil and Paraguay are relatively high-interest-rate countries. Uruguay is in an in-between situation. On the whole, Table 2.2 suggests that convergence amongst the MERCOSUR countries does not appear to be in sight.

Macroeconomic convergence targets were approved in the year 2000 by the

Table 2.3 *Convergence criteria – MERCOSUR data*

Year	Inflation (consumer prices)				Government budget/GDP[a]				Government debt/GDP[b]				Bal.payments current account/GDP			
	Argentina	Brazil	Paraguay	Uruguay	Argentina	Brazil	Paraguay	Uruguay	Argentina	Brazil	Paraguay	Uruguay	Argentina	Brazil	Paraguay	Urugauy
1991	84.0	480.2	11.8	81.3	-0.5	-0.1	-0.2	1.2	45.8	36.9	26.2	41.2	-0.3	-0.3	-5.2	-0.1
1992	17.6	1157.8	17.8	59.0	0.6	-1.8	-0.6	1.5	37.2	38.2	19.4	34.9	-2.4	1.6	-0.9	-1.9
1993	7.4	2708.2	20.4	52.9	1.2	-0.7	0.4	-0.6	34.6	32.8	17.7	31.1	-3.4	-0.1	-0.9	-2.9
1994	3.9	1093.9	18.3	44.1	-0.1	1.1	1.1	-2.2	34.7	28.5	15.9	30.5	-4.3	-0.3	-3.5	-2.3
1995	1.6	14.8	10.5	35.4	-0.5	-5.0	-0.3	-1.4	37.9	31.6	14.8	28.8	-1.9	-2.6	-3.1	-1.1
1996	0.1	9.3	8.2	24.3	-1.9	-3.8	-1.1	-1.5	40.8	33.3	13.9	28.1	-2.4	-3.0	-5.2	-1.1
1997	0.3	7.5	6.2	15.2	-1.5	-4.3	-1.4	-1.4	39.4	34.5	15.1	28.4	-4.1	-3.8	-2.5	-1.3
1998	0.7	1.7	14.6	8.6	-1.4	-7.5	-1.0	-1.0	39.0	42.4	18.9	26.9	-4.8	-4.3	-1.7	-2.1
1999	-1.8	19.9	5.4	4.2	-1.7	-10.0	-1.0	-3.8	42.3	46.9	24.8	27.5	-4.3	-4.6	-1.8	-2.9
2000	-0.9	9.8	9.0	4.8	-2.4	-4.6	-3.6	-4.1	47.5	47.7	33.1	28.7	-3.2	-4.1	-1.4	-3.0

Notes:
[a] Government budget: primary result plus operational result plus public companies result.
[b] Government debt includes federal debt and the debt of states/provinces and municipalities.

Source: As for Table 2.2.

Presidents of the MERCOSUR countries. Giambiagi (1999) also suggested similar targets. Both sets of proposals can be put together and summarized as follows. Member countries, and any other South American countries aspiring to join MERCOSUR, would be required to adhere to the following: (i) a free trade area should be created; (ii) member countries would have to harmonize their criteria for defining and measuring the principal macroeconomic variables; (iii) member countries should not devalue their currencies and they would have to maintain their exchange rates within the margins to be determined; (iv) the annual inflation rate in a specific country should not exceed 3.0 per cent; (v) any member country's budget deficit should not exceed 3.0 per cent of GDP; (vi) the net public sector debt of any member country of MERCOSUR should not exceed 40.0 per cent of GDP; and (vii) member countries should not have excessive current account deficits, where a maximum of 3.0 per cent of GDP was thought appropriate.

We may begin our commentary with the first point: the creation of a free trade area. MERCOSUR is far from creating a free trade area due to trade conflicts, basically, between Argentina and Brazil. Giambiagi (1999), for instance, argues that there is a deterioration in trade relations within the MERCOSUR area: 'problems such as those that affected the sugar sector in Argentina, or the protest against Brazilian phytosanitary controls . . . [A]fter the devaluation of the real, Argentine producers made . . . demands, such as the introduction of a specific tariff against Brazilian goods, safeguard measures and the establishment of quotas' (p. 20).

In terms of the criteria for defining and measuring the principal macroeconomic variables and the maintenance of a more stable exchange rate, despite some attempts at harmonizing the main macroeconomic variables, at least up to now no more progress can be reported. As for a stable exchange rate region, this may be difficult to achieve in view of the fact that Brazil and Argentina, the most important partners of MERCOSUR, had, until recently, different monetary and exchange rate regimes. Even though the exchange regimes of the MERCOSUR countries differ a little among themselves, it will be difficult to adopt some plan of macroeconomic coordination and eventually a monetary union. Moreover, it is important to stress two points: on the one hand, the sharp and quick devaluation of the Brazilian real, in 2001, by around 20.5 per cent, created serious difficulties between Brazil and Argentina, since the latter could not devalue its currency to compensate for the movements of the real. On the other hand, after devaluing its currency, in January 2002, Argentina witnessed an overshooting exchange rate process. The dollar–peso was on a one-for-one basis at the beginning of 2002; one month and a half later, it had jumped to 2.0 pesos per dollar. Thus the new exchange rate and monetary regime in Argentina will bring some macroeconomic instability to MERCOSUR, at least in the near future. In other words, the different monetary and

Lessons from EMU for MERCOSUR

exchange rate regimes in these countries can be very disruptive. Fanelli (2000) puts it aptly when he argues that 'it is almost impossible to imagine that countries adopt macroeconomic co-ordination ignoring completely the existing type of exchange rate regime' (p. 3; original in Spanish).

The experience of the fixed rate regime which tied the Argentine peso on a one-for-one basis to the dollar provides a warning of the consequences of a monetary union between countries with different economic circumstances and policies and without the structure for the coordination of economic policies. The peso–dollar link was entered on a unilateral basis for Argentina and, unlike the full monetary union of EMU under the euro, it was reversible (as the Argentine crisis of January 2002 shows). But that peso–dollar experience serves to illustrate the difficulties which arise from lack of similar inflationary conditions and the deflationary effects which can result from a poorly designed (quasi-) monetary union. Our analysis in section 5 is pertinent in this context.

We concentrate on Table 2.3 to assess the rest of the conditions referred to above. Concerning the inflation rate target, despite the substantial reduction in the inflation rates in Argentina, Brazil, Paraguay and Uruguay, especially since 1998, these countries still have inflation rates above the 3.0 per cent threshold, with the exception of Argentina, which has had an inflation rate under 3.0 per cent since 1995. However, the ceiling of 3 per cent of inflation for each country may be too ambitious if one considers the high past inflation rates in the countries of the region. Argentina is the only country that had in the second half of the 1990s an inflation rate below 3 per cent, but this was only possible with the adoption of an extremely rigid currency board regime. But then Argentina is the country with the highest rate of unemployment in the MERCOSUR area (see Table 2.2).

The figures for the fiscal deficits in MERCOSUR countries show that: (a) the fiscal deficit in Brazil, since 1995, has been greater than 3.0 per cent of GDP; (b) Argentina's budget deficit, between 1991 and 2000, was always less than the target established; and (c) fiscal deficits in Paraguay and Uruguay have been less than 3.0 per cent of GDP throughout except for 2000, and for 1999 and 2000, respectively. In terms of the ratio of public sector debt to GDP we observe that: (a) in the case of Paraguay over the period 1991–2000, it has been less than 40.0 per cent, although it has increased in the last three years; in Uruguay, from 1991 to 2000, it has been satisfied, but it has been increasing since 1999; (b) in Argentina it was greater than 40.0 per cent in 1999 and 2000; and in Brazil during the last three years, it has been greater than 40.0 per cent, and it has been increasing. Finally, looking at the figures relating to the current account deficits, it may be noted that, in 2000, the ratio of current account deficit to GDP is above 3 per cent for Argentina and Brazil, but below that level for Paraguay, and just under 3 per cent in the case of Uruguay. It is also important to note that since 1996 there has been a clear deterioration in the current account deficit of Argentina, Brazil and Uruguay, and this tendency has been followed, mainly in the case of Argentina and Brazil, by an increase in the foreign debt to GDP ratio (see Table 2.2). This raises an intriguing question in that given these high foreign debt to GDP ratios, the 3.0 per cent and 40.0 per cent fiscal criteria, even though they may not be so restrictive, cannot be feasible. When external pressures oblige central banks to raise their interest rates sharply, government debt would inevitably increase in view of the short-term maturity of securities in the MERCOSUR area.

We summarize by suggesting that the attempt to create a MERCOSUR regional monetary union is open to a number of objections: first, MERCOSUR's factor markets are not sufficiently unified to make it an optimum currency area; second, the volume of intra-regional trade among the MERCOSUR countries is still low; and the macroeconomic variables in the proposed union show that there is a long way to go before convergence is achieved. We thus concur with Eichengreen (2000) that MERCOSUR countries do not appear to satisfy the preconditions for a monetary union.

7. SUMMARY AND CONCLUSIONS

We have argued in this chapter that the use of the EMU model of monetary union implies adopting a deflationary policy. Since the countries of MERCO-SUR have more social problems than the countries of the EU, the cost of adopting a MERCOSUR monetary union on the euro pattern would probably be greater than in the case of the EU. It would be necessary to have much more flexible mechanisms of compensation in terms of fiscal transfers in order to tackle the socioeconomic problems of the MERCOSUR countries. This would be difficult even in the medium to long run if one considers the magnitude of the fiscal problems in these countries. Consequently, the first lesson that can be drawn from the EMU experience is to avoid using this model as the benchmark for a possible MERCOSUR monetary union.

Our analysis also shows that there is no evidence that macroeconomic convergence is evident in MERCOSUR. The area has only minimally achieved some basic criteria defined by the OCA literature, and as Eichengreen (2000) argues, 'the list of preconditions for a single currency to operate smoothly is rather formidable, and it is not clear that the members of MERCOSUR union are prepared to satisfy them' (p. 19). Besides, the macroeconomic problems the MERCOSUR countries are faced with are so big that even in the long run it is difficult to believe that some minimum convergence can be reached. A monetary union requires achieving some convergence in terms of preferences between inflation and unemployment, among other macroeconomic variables. Although the process of democracy is consolidating in the Southern countries of Latin America, they are still too far from a balanced political system, mainly in the two bigger countries, Brazil and Argentina. Consequently, it will be difficult for the MERCOSUR countries to reach a consensus in terms of both an economic and a political agenda.

It is still too early to evaluate the effects of exchange rate devaluation in Argentina, in terms of inflation, GDP growth and balance of payments accounts, and so on, since this change is very recent. Indeed, a context of macroeconomic instability is not appropriate to set up new macroeconomic convergence targets. However, it is likely that, in the future, the adoption of a floating exchange regime by Argentina may favour MERCOSUR countries to adopt more effective mechanisms of macroeconomic coordination.

A final comment relates to the fact that since MERCOSUR has not even reached the stage of a common market yet, it is premature to think of the countries composing it as being ready to form a monetary union. It is indeed the case that 'supplementing regional integration with an initiative to stabilize the exchange rate or move toward a single currency becomes more urgent when integration moves beyond the establishment of a free trade area or a custom union to the creation of a deeply integrated market' (Eichengreen, 2000, p. 21), so that 'monetary union makes sense as a solution to MERCOSUR's exchange regime rate problem only if it is part of a significantly deeper project' (ibid., p. 44). It is thus premature to discuss a MERCOSUR monetary union. Above all, however, even if the stage were reached for such a union, we would suggest that the EMU model is not appropriate for this area.

NOTES

* This chapter was originally presented to the Workshop entitled 'Towards Macroeconomic Convergence in MERCOSUR? Lessons from the European Monetary Union', organized by the Centre for Brazilian Studies and Argentine Studies Programme, University of Oxford, and held at St Antony's College, University of Oxford, 12 June 2001. The chapter was updated, in February 2002, to account for the turbulence in Argentina.
1. As is well known, the Convertibility Plan, implemented in April 1991, established by law a one-to-one parity between the Argentine currency, the peso, and the US dollar. It also required the currency in circulation to be equal to the available gold and currency reserves. As a result, the Central Bank of Argentina became a 'currency board'. For an analysis of the Convertibility Plan, see Fanelli et al. (1996).
2. It is important to note that, from December 2001 to January 2002, after the former president Fernando de la Rua was forced to resign due to his own mistakes, Argentina had three different presidents.
3. Incidentally, it was called a 'Little Maastricht' for the MERCOSUR.
4. In 1991 and 2000 the relation between total 'fob exports' of Argentina, Brazil, Paraguay and Uruguay and total GDP of these countries was 0.80 per cent and 1.92 per cent, respectively. The intra-regional exports of MERCOSUR countries, in 1991 and 2000, represented 10.80 per cent and 20.30 per cent of total exports of MERCOSUR countries to the rest of the world, respectively. The figures just cited are own calculations from CEPAL/ECLAC (www.cepal.org).

5. In this particular context, the theory of OCA shows that the greater the asymmetry of output movements, the higher the value placed on changes in the exchange rate as an instrument of relative price adjustment.

REFERENCES

Arestis, P. and M. Sawyer (1998), 'New Labour, New Monetarism', *Soundings*, Vol. 9, Summer, reprinted in *European Labour Forum*, Vol. 20, Winter, 1998–99.

Arestis, P., Brown, A. and Sawyer, M. (2001), *The Euro: Evolution and Prospects*, Cheltenham, UK and Northampton, USA: Edward Elgar Publishing.

Arestis, P., McCauley, K. and Sawyer, M. (2001), 'An Alternative Stability and Growth Pact for the European Union', *Cambridge Journal of Economics*, Vol. 25, No. 1, pp. 113–30.

Arestis, P., Biefang-Frisancho Mariscal, I., Brown, A. and Sawyer, M. (2002), 'Explaining the Euro's Initial Decline', *Eastern Economic Journal*, Vol. 28, No. 1, pp. 71–88.

CEPAL/ECLAC (2001), http://www.cepal.org.

Edwards, S. (1998), 'How About a Single Currency for MERCOSUR?' *Wall Street Journal*, 28 August, p. A11.

Eichengreen, B. (2000), 'Does MERCOSUR Need a Single Currency?', in IPEA (ed.), *Mercosur and the Free Trade Areas of the Americas*, Vol. 1, Brasília: IPEA.

Fanelli, J.M. (2000), *Coordinación Macroeconómica en el Mercosur: Marco Analítico y Hechos Estilizados*, Buenos Aires: CEDES, November.

Fanelli, J.M., Rozenwurcel, G. and Simpson, L. (1996), *Financial Liberalization in Developing Countries: the Argentine Experience in the Nineties*, Buenos Aires: CEDES.

Ferrari-Filho, F. (2002), 'A Critique of the Proposal of Monetary Union in Mercosur', in Paul Davidson (ed.), *A Post Keynesian Perspective on Twenty-First Century Economic Problems*, Cheltenham, UK and Northampton, USA: Edward Elgar Publishing, pp. 56–68.

Financial Times (1998), 23 March.

Giambiagi, F. (1999), 'Mercosur: Why Does Monetary Union Make Sense in the Long Run?', *Ensaios BNDES*, Vol. 12, December, Rio de Janeiro.

Inter-American Development Bank (2001), http://www.iadb.org.

Kenen, P. (1969), 'The Theory of Optimum Currency Areas: an Eclectic View', in R. Mundell and A. Swoboda (eds), *Monetary Problems of the International Economy*, Chicago: University of Chicago Press.

McKinnon, R.I. (1963), 'Optimum Currency Areas', *American Economic Review*, Vol. 53, No. 4, pp. 717–25.

Meirelles, A.C. (1999), 'Tamanho É Documento na Competição Bancária', *Forum de Lideres/Gazeta Mercantil*, Vol. 1, No. 1, pp. 54–72.

Mercosul (2001), http://www.mercosul.org.

Mundell, R.A. (1961), 'A Theory of Optimal Currency Areas', *American Economic Review*, Vol. 53, No. 1, pp. 657–64.

Paula, L.F.R. (1998), 'Tamanho, Dimensão e Concentração do Sistema Bancário no Contexto de Alta e Baixa Inflação no Brasil', *Nova Economia*, Vol. 8, No. 1, pp. 87–116.

Paula, L.F.R., Sobreira, R. and Zonenschain, C.N. (eds) (1999), *Perspectivas para o Sistema Financeiro Nacional: Regulação do Setor e Participação do Capital Estrangeiro*, Rio de Janeiro, Universidade Candido Mendes-Ipanema.

Pentecost, E.J. (1999), 'Monetary Unions in Nineteenth Century Europe: An Historical Perspective and Lessons for EMU in the Twenty-first Century', in S. Daniel, P. Arestis and J. Grahl (eds), *The History and Practice of Economics, Essays in Honour of B. Corry and M. Peston*, Vol. 2, Cheltenham, UK and Northampton, USA: Edward Elgar Publishers.

Rigolon, F. and Giambiagi, F. (1999), 'Áreas Monetárias Ótimas: Teoria, Unificação Monetária Européia e Aplicações para o Mercosul', *Economia Aplicada*, Vol. 3, No. 1, pp. 79–99.

Valdovinos, C.G.F. (2000), 'Cyclical Co-Movements in Output Across MERCOSUR Countries', http://www.bcp.gov.py/GEE/investman/carlos/cyclical.htm.

PART II

MERCOSUR Macroeconomic Policy
Coordination

3. MERCOSUR: why does monetary union make sense in the long term?*

Fabio Giambiagi

1. INTRODUCTION[1]

In May 1997, Barry Eichengreen, one of the most important authorities on global monetary issues, wrote an article on free trade in which he refers to the idea of creating a single currency in MERCOSUR. He states: 'This is unrealistic . . . over any horizon relevant for policy planning' since, in contrast to the intensity of European integration, '*nothing similar is likely to occur in our lifetimes in South America*' (Eichengreen, 1997, p. 31, emphasis added).

It is a common reaction to most observers when they first face the idea of monetary union in MERCOSUR. However, if the question is analyzed in depth, the conclusions that emerge may differ greatly. In fact, even Eichengreen (1998), in an article written specifically on this issue one year later, and interestingly called 'Does MERCOSUR Need a Single Currency?', expressed an opinion markedly different from the previous one. He acknowledged that 'there is a coherent political-economy logic for why the members of the customs union might contemplate a common currency' (Eichengreen, 1998, p. 4) and, in what concerns the countries of the subregion, he stated that 'if they intend to press on to deeper integration, then they, like their European counterparts, will also have to contemplate monetary integration' (p. 10). Moreover, after asserting that 'the option of monetary union cannot be ruled out as infeasible a priori' (p. 25), Eichengreen concluded, in contrast to the totally skeptical view expressed a year before:

> If [integration] . . . develops a readiness to transform MERCOSUR into a more far-reaching integration initiative, involving the creation of a true single, integrated South American market, then exchange rate swings will become more politically disruptive, and monetary unification becomes *not only feasible but essential*. (p. 33, emphasis added)

How did this idea emerge? In all processes of economic subregional integration there is a natural sequence to be followed. It begins with the establishment of a free trade area (FTA), then the introduction of a common external tariff (CET), and, finally, the creation of a common market. The common market is characterized by the constitution of a geographic area in which the countries, while preserving their own laws and political organization, agree to harmonize their respective legislation in certain areas, coordinate their macroeconomic policies and, in general, allow the 'four freedoms': the free circulation of goods, services, labor and capital. At a later stage, the common market could also include monetary union. Western Europe, or at least most of it, is about to start this 'fourth stage' of integration – that is, the establishment of monetary union. This will take place after the physical substitution of the national currencies of the countries involved by the currency of the European Monetary Union (EMU) – the euro – in 2002.

The Treaty of Asunción, which gave rise to MERCOSUR, anticipates a sequence of events similar to that discussed above, although there is no reference to monetary union. Article 1 of MERCOSUR's founding treaty thus states that

> the member states agree to create a common market that . . . will be called the 'Southern Common Market' (*Mercado Común del Sur*, MERCOSUR). This common market implies: the free circulation of goods, services, and productive factors between the countries . . .; the establishment of a common external tariff and the adoption of a common trade policy in relation to third countries . . .; macroeconomic and sectoral policy coordination between the member states, including foreign trade, agricultural, industrial, *fiscal, monetary, exchange rate, and capital policy* . . .' (Emphasis added)

However, although the treaty was signed and the FTA and CET were defined and initiated many years ago, despite some problems, little or no progress has been made toward the creation of a common market.[2]

This loss of dynamism in regional integration implies two types of problems for the future of MERCOSUR. First, 'in a competitive and dynamic world where productive investment is in dispute, by not *advancing or advancing quickly the process is reversed*' (Lavagna, 1996, p. 2, emphasis added).[3] Second, if MERCOSUR limits itself to an FTA with a CET, its strength will be significantly diminished when the Free Trade Area of the Americas (FTAA) is established. This is because, once tariffs disappear in the Americas, the ability of the subregion to distinguish itself from the rest of the countries will naturally be undermined. In other words, for MERCOSUR to conserve its strength once the FTAA is established, the former should be far more than a free trade area with a common external tariff.

Taking these arguments into consideration, a discussion about the possibility of establishing a single currency for the MERCOSUR countries, perhaps in the second decade of the twenty-first century, began in 1997. For this to occur, however, the countries would have to make arrangements in advance (Giambiagi, 1997, 1998; Lavagna and Giambiagi, 1998; Rigolon and Giambiagi, 1999). This idea was first raised in a press article published in the *Estado de São Paulo* on 8 April 1997 ('A Proposal for MERCOSUR'), which summarized a purely academic article by Giambiagi (1997). This idea gained political momentum when it was included in MERCOSUR's diplomatic agenda after being mentioned by Argentine President Carlos Menem in a press interview on 27 April 1997. Menem made further references to the proposal on numerous occasions. The idea thus began to be identified as an Argentine proposal. The Argentine government even held an international seminar on the issue in Buenos Aires in June 1998.[4] At the same time, the MERCOSUR authorities began to discuss it, although informally, after it was mentioned in statements made by some Argentine authorities.[5] Examining this issue so much in advance may appear rather unrealistic, but taking global geopolitical considerations into account, such anticipation is reasonable and constitutes part of the countries' strategic vision in this respect.[6]

In a way, this type of logic has also influenced European integration *vis-à-vis* the creation of the euro. It was seen as an incentive for the EMU member states to make greater efforts to advance in areas where progress had been slow – such as in cooperation and mutual understanding – despite Europe's long history of integration. This was acknowledged by Jaques Delors, one of the mentors of monetary union: 'In the longer run, *European Monetary Union should also promote the partial harmonization of national tax and labor policies*. In other words, the virtuous cycle now underway should lead, via a single currency, to still further economic integration' (Delors, 1997, p. 17, emphasis added).

This study is divided into nine sections. After this introduction, prospects for MERCOSUR after the possible establishment of the FTAA are examined. Interpretations of the origins and logic guiding the European unification proposal, via the 1992 Maastricht Treaty – which influenced MERCOSUR's proposal for monetary union – will then be analyzed. Section 4 highlights the prerequisites that are generally viewed as fundamental for the creation of a monetary union. Section 5 analyzes recent trends towards greater macroeconomic convergence in the MERCOSUR countries. Section 6 examines developments since 1997, when the first informal discussions on the idea of monetary union began. This section is followed by a defense of this unification proposal, in the context of MERCOSUR, as a long-term project for the subregion. Section 8 examines the dollarization proposal as an alternative to the above-mentioned proposal for unification. Finally, a working agenda for the 2000–2002 period is examined.

2.   MERCOSUR AND THE CHALLENGE OF THE FTAA

In the last few years, the unity of MERCOSUR has been undermined by events such as Argentina's opposition to Brazil's candidacy for a place on the UN Security Council; the criticism of prominent Brazilian political leaders of what they saw as closer ties between Argentina and the USA, to the detriment of its regional partners; the Argentine Congress's approval of a law preventing the application of preferential tariffs on Brazilian sugar imports to Argentina; the retaliatory measures of Brazilian political leaders, through an initiative by the President of MERCOSUR's Parliamentary Commission, consisting of a legislative decree bill that banned the import of Argentine wheat and so forth. It is highly unlikely that these problems would have had the fertile ground to flourish had MERCOSUR been in a phase of continuous progress, as in the first half of the 1990s. These issues suggest the existence of an 'adolescent crisis' in MERCOSUR, which should define what future it wants.

The succession of frictions and the increasing unwillingness to make any concessions to integration highlight the need to discuss the future of MERCO-SUR once an FTA and a CET are established among its member states. The fact that these frictions occurred emphasizes the need to upgrade MERCO-SUR so that it ceases to be a mere trade agreement and, continuing to deepen integration, makes progress towards the creation of a truly common market. To a certain extent, MERCOSUR is at a crossroads.[7] One possibility, alternative A, would be to view the progress made thus far as satisfactory and to say that no further progress should be made. In this respect, alternative B would consist of making a leap forward and of identifying new areas of integration, with the underlying advantage of definitively consolidating trade integration.

Alternative A implies adopting a passive approach, although there are serious problems associated with it:

> if MERCOSUR is limited to a free trade area with a common external tariff, its strength will be severely diminished once the FTAA is established, because as soon as tariffs are eliminated in the three Americas – North, Central and South – the ability of the subregion to distinguish itself from the rest of the countries in the continent will naturally be undermined. That is, for MERCOSUR to maintain its strength once the FTAA is established, it should become far more than an FTA. In other words, if its member states are incapable of deepening the agreement, the creation of the FTAA represents, in practice, the death of MERCOSUR.

Under this first alternative, MERCOSUR would be a bloc with scant supra-nationality, diluted in a larger free trade area. MERCOSUR would thus be left with few policy-making powers *vis-à-vis* the large multinationals and the hegemonic global centers.

Alternative B, associated with a more dynamic approach, implies that

MERCOSUR will still play an important role characterized as: (i) a response to the question of what its global role would be in 10 or 20 year's time; (ii) a medium-sized economic power *vis-à-vis* the large blocs consisting of NAFTA (North American Free Trade Area), the European Union and the Asian countries, with a consolidated supranational dimension, representing one kind of power in the new world order; and (iii) an affirmation of regional identity, in all its aspects – economic, geopolitical and cultural. This alternative would be far more arduous, since it would demand negotiations in a number of areas and the development of an extensive working agenda, as well as the diplomatic effort implied by the FTAA process. However, it would avoid the risks associated with alternative A.

This dynamic approach in favor of integration, regardless of whether a single currency is introduced as the final stage of the process, should result in concrete progress being made over the next few years, such as (a) establishing mechanisms for macroeconomic coordination between countries, without which the barriers to intra-subregional trade integration could proliferate; (b) further studies of the creation of a common citizenship, through the introduction of a MERCOSUR passport; (c) a joint effort by the countries of the subregion to harmonize, for example, their tax, labor and capital market legislation.

If this more dynamic approach is not adopted, in an extreme case, as Argentina, Brazil, Paraguay and Uruguay eventually decide to join the other parallel processes of trade liberalization that are making good progress, the question 'what is MERCOSUR for?' will become unanswerable and the bloc will lose its raison d'étre. The next section will examine the conditions that MERCOSUR must meet to continue as a separate entity in the context of the new global environment of the next few decades.

3. THE PARALLELS WITH MAASTRICHT: A TAXONOMY OF THE INTERPRETATIONS OF THE VALIDITY OF THE EUROPEAN SINGLE CURRENCY

The natural source of inspiration for the proposal concerning monetary union in MERCOSUR is Europe, which introduced the euro as a fiduciary currency in 1999. The euro will become an exchange mechanism, substituting national currencies, in 2002. In respect of the process of European integration, Schweickert, Zahler and Jessen have indicated that 'the early start of the Economic and Monetary Union and the creation of a single currency serves as a splendid *learning opportunity* for Latin American and Caribbean countries engaged in regional or subregional integration schemes' (Schweickert, Zahler and Jessen, 1997, p. 30, emphasis in the original). Therefore, it is useful to identify the factors that determined this process and the parallels that can be made with the MERCOSUR countries. There are several interpretations in relation to the reasons behind the agreement to establish monetary union that resulted in the 1992 Maastricht Treaty.

3.1   A Solution for the Inconsistencies Associated with Incomplete Integration

According to this interpretation, monetary union is the natural solution for the problems arising from incomplete integration – that is, without monetary integration – and a mechanism for improving the efficiency of the economies that constitute an FTA. According to Giavazzi and Giovannini (1991), 'the survival of the current system of fixed but adjustable parities must be ascribed to the operation of capital controls. However, capital controls prevent financial integration. Thus, *financial integration requires that European countries give up realignments altogether, moving toward a system of credible, and thus irrevocably fixed, exchange rate. This is a monetary union*' (emphasis added). At the same time, according to this view, monetary union would be nothing more than the logical outcome of the prior process of integration. This is the origin of the 'one market, one money' principle set out by the European Economic Community a few years before Maastricht (ECC, 1990).[8]

3.2   A Mechanism for Preventing Reverses in the Integration Process

This view is supported by, among others, Collignon et al., 1994:

> In the long run, distortions in the structure of relative prices misdirect the use of resources and draw capital and labour into uses which remain profitable only so long as inflation accelerates. This effect is damaging for the functioning of the economy . . . The same applies to instability resulting from exchange rate instability in the Single Market. The uncertainty which dominates market relations based on different currencies introduces the need for hedging operations and drives a distorting wedge between prices, which leads to a misallocation of resources. *An integrated market, where goods and services are allowed to circulate freely and information is readily available, but where the value of commodities is expressed in separate currencies, is therefore necessarily suboptimal and could disintegrate again* if distortions turn welfare gains into losses . . . Only with full economic and monetary union and a single currency will the informational distortions that are implicit in a multicurrency standard be eliminated . . . [for] . . . achieve a truly efficient and Single Market' (pp. 89–90, emphasis in the original)

With the development of the European 'snake' mechanism of exchange rate parities in the European Community at the end of the 1980s, the latter reached a crossroads, since the internal logic of unification required the abolition of capital controls. However, this would have caused greater exchange rate volatility in Europe. Thus, Western Europe had to choose between exchange rate flexibility or monetary union. Even the early critics of EMU recognized that

> wider exchange rate swings would compound the adjustment difficulties associated with completing Europe's internal market. If national industries – under pressure from the removal of barriers to intra-European trade – find their competitive position eroded further by a sudden exchange rate appreciation, resistance to the implementation of the Single European Act (SEA) would intensify. The SEA might be repudiated. *In this sense and this sense alone, monetary unification is a logical economic corollary of factor – and product – integration.* (Eichengreen, 1993, p. 1331, emphasis added)[9]

3.3 An Opportunity to Secure Greater Credibility

This interpretation is based on the following premises: (i) low inflation is a positive long-term condition for economic growth; (ii) the aim of achieving and maintaining low inflation requires consistent fiscal and monetary policies; (iii) the success of such policies is associated with an institutional environment that allows economic policy decisions to be isolated from the demands of the political cycle. EMU is thus a mechanism that 'ties the hands' of the countries of the agreement. It even serves as an 'alibi' when these adopt unpopular measures, since the 'blame' falls on an external agent of that country. In certain respects, this is equivalent to 'exporting' the Bundesbank's credibility to the other countries that, together with Germany, make up the monetary union. This point of view is held by, among others, Giavazzi and Pagano (1988) (before the Maastricht Treaty), as well as by Sandholtz (1993). In respect of the increase in credibility conferred on those national policies direct toward fighting inflation – understood as the most efficient basis for long-term growth – Sandholtz (1993) notes that

> European governments favored European Monetary Union because it would provide the highest possible level of credibility; . . . monetary union would be more credible than unilateral pegging to a strong currency because the latter could be undone at any time, even in response to temporary electoral concerns. In fact, monetary union would provide price stability for governments that would be unable, for domestic policy reasons, to achieve it on their own.

This view was subsequently backed up by the following: 'For governments that found it difficult domestically to achieve monetary discipline, European Monetary Union offered the chance to have it implemented from without. *Governments could even escape the blame when tight monetary policies pinched* (ibid., p. 38, emphasis added).

3.4   A Combination of Complementary National Interests

This interpretation highlights a combination of complementary national interests that led to the decision to create EMU. On the one hand, a group of European countries, led by France, was interested in weakening the domination of Germany in the economic decision making that affected their economic performance. In practice, in the period of the Maastricht Agreement, all of the countries of Western Europe were subordinate to German monetary policy. Establishing an EMU in which all the countries affected by this policy would be represented was a way of sharing responsibility for European monetary policy. In parallel (and this helps to understand not only the support of these countries, but principally German backing for the agreement), monetary union – after the fall of the Berlin Wall and specifically in the context of German unification – was a mechanism for guaranteeing European peace and unity and of assuring the rest of Western Europe that Germany would continue to be part of the same bloc and would preserve the communitarian spirit that marked the postwar European integration process. At the same time, Germany's loyalty to the integrationist philosophy during the initial negotiations on EMU obviated the danger that France would use its political veto to block German unification. The then President of the Bundesbank, Helmut Schlesinger, acknowledged that EMU would not have significant economic benefits for Germany and that German support for the project was strictly political in nature.

Some of the incentives evident in the European experience are not present in the case of MERCOSUR, although others assume greater importance. In particular, the problems associated with incomplete integration did not have the same consequences as outlined in subsection 3.1 and there is nothing that comes close to matching the concerns in Europe over German expansionism, as mentioned in subsection 3.4. However, the risks of an incomplete integration process reversing itself, as described in subsection 3.2, are real and the commitment to stability associated with institutional change, as highlighted in subsection 3.3, has potentially many more benefits – in terms of a reduction of interest rates and the creation of a favorable environment for investment – for Latin American countries, which struggle against a track record of high inflation, in contrast to Europe's decades-long history of low inflation.

4.   THE NECESSARY CONDITIONS FOR INTRODUCING A SINGLE CURRENCY[10]

The introduction of a single currency should be associated with a *latu sensu* single market. This means, among other things, that the labor market formed by the geographic space using the same currency is characterized by mobility of factors, thus avoiding differences in unemployment rates. In practice, however, this is difficult to achieve, and sometimes even within countries it is possible to find markedly different regional unemployment rates. Nevertheless, in theory, the literature on optimal currency areas (OCAs) emphasizes the following necessary aspects to justify the creation of a single currency:[11]

1. Free movement of labor factors between countries. This makes it possible to react to external shocks in a uniform manner. The constraints to this mobility include legal, economic and cultural factors such as language. The most important economic factor concerns the difficulty of harmonizing national pensions systems and validating in the other countries the contributions made by each worker in their country of origin.
2. High level of intra-regional trade. Countries that do not trade with each other have no incentive to adopt a single currency. By contrast, if 100 per cent of the trade of a group of countries is intra-subregional, monetary union is practically a precondition. After decades of integration, Europe has increased its intra-subregional trade, this being one of the most important factors in favor of integration.
3. Similarities in the types of shock that affect a group of countries. A region which, for example, consists of large oil importers as well as important oil exporters is not a good candidate for monetary integration, since variations in the price of oil affect these countries in opposite ways. On the other hand, countries with similar features tend to confront shocks in the same manner and are therefore, according to this point of view, good candidates for monetary union.[12]

Therefore, an optimal exchange rate area – defined as a geographic space well suited to adopting a single currency – is one in which the countries that are included in it share characteristics that make them vulnerable to the same types of shock, 'so that policies that are generally appropriate in one country are also appropriate for other member countries' (Englander and Egebo, 1993, p. 11).

It is precisely this factor that makes labor market flexibility in the countries involved in monetary union especially important. As Englander and Egebo (1993) again stress:

> with exchange rates fixed, the option of changing relative prices quickly via nominal exchange rate changes is not available. Hence, real exchange-rate adjustments, when needed, must be achieved through changes in relative costs and prices. However, if wages and prices are not flexible internally and credibility effects do not greatly affect wage and price decisions, such adjustment may require large shifts in capacity utilization and employment. In general, *the greater the degree of wage*

and price rigidity, the more the output and employment response that would be needed to alter relative prices. (p. 9, emphasis added)

At the same time, as highlighted by Bovenberg et al. (1991), the fact that the mobility of the labor factor is limited, and that there is a certain rigidity of prices and wages, implies that once the possibility of changing intra-sub-regional exchange rate parities disappears from a group of countries in a monetary union the member countries of the agreement need to have some flexibility in their respective fiscal policies. They can thus combat future shocks that could affect them in different ways.

In this context, what is the situation of the MERCOSUR countries? The motives behind their possible adoption of monetary union lies fundamentally in the strengthening of an institutional environment that nurtures long-term price stabilization – including a single and independent central bank; the setting of limits on the relationship between the fiscal deficit and GDP; and in having low inflation targets. Regardless of this, however, there is evidence that certain conditions necessary for the creation of a monetary union are gradually being met, while others are not. After 1991, intra-subregional trade grew more rapidly than trade with the rest of the world. In particular, MERCOSUR's two largest economies, Brazil and Argentina, have an external sector with relatively similar characteristics in terms of their dependence on external capital flows. They thus tend to be equally sensitive to fluctuations in the international prices of their export goods, to world economic growth, external interest rates and/or the liquidity conditions of the international financial market. There are also many issues on which MERCOSUR must make progress. These will be discussed in a subsequent section.

5. MACROECONOMIC CONVERGENCE IN THE MERCOSUR COUNTRIES

In the last few years, the process of macroeconomic convergence of the MERCOSUR countries – understood as the increasing similarity in the performance of the various economies of the subregion – has deepened. This is an important factor when considering the unification of their currencies.

Table 3.1 supports what was previously noted about the growing similarity of certain performance indicators in the Argentine, Brazilian, Paraguayan and Uruguayan economies. These figures show GDP growth rates over the last five decades and, in the last line, their standard deviation (SD) in each year.[13] Figure 3.1 was drawn on the basis of the last line of this table.

Figure 3.1 presents the running mean – for ten-year periods – of the SD in the GDP growth rates of the MERCOSUR countries. Therefore, the values included in these correspond to the arithmetic mean for 10-year running periods of the

Table 3.1   GDP growth rates of the MERCOSUR countries (percentages)

	1947	1948	1949	1950	1951	1952	1953	1954	1955	1956	1957	1958	1959	1960	1961	1962	1963	1964
Argentina	3.7	1.2	-4.6	1.6	3.9	-5.1	5.4	4.1	7.1	2.8	5.1	6.1	-6.4	7.8	7.1	-1.6	-2.4	10.3
Brazil	2.4	7.4	6.6	6.5	5.9	8.7	2.5	10.1	6.9	3.1	8.1	7.7	5.5	9.8	10.3	5.2	1.6	2.9
Paraguay	-13.1	1.1	16.8	-1.7	1.9	-1.7	2.8	1.7	4.6	4.2	4.6	5.7	0.4	0.1	4.8	7.0	2.7	4.3
Uruguay	6.7	2.6	3.7	3.1	8.2	-0.4	6.5	5.7	1.6	1.7	1.0	-3.6	-2.8	3.5	2.9	-2.2	0.5	2.0
Standard deviation	8.87	2.96	8.83	3.40	2.70	5.89	1.96	3.54	2.56	1.03	2.91	5.12	5.05	4.35	3.19	4.68	2.19	3.74

	1965	1966	1967	1968	1969	1970	1971	1972	1973	1974	1975	1976	1977	1978	1979	1980	1981	1982
Argentina	9.1	0.6	2.7	4.3	8.6	5.4	4.8	3.1	6.1	6.5	-1.4	-2.9	6.4	-3.4	6.7	0.7	-6.2	-4.2
Brazil	2.7	3.8	4.9	11.2	9.9	8.8	13.3	11.7	13.9	9.8	5.7	9.2	4.7	5.0	6.4	7.2	-1.6	0.6
Paraguay	5.7	1.1	6.3	3.6	3.9	6.2	4.4	5.1	7.8	8.3	4.8	7.1	12.7	11.3	11.4	11.4	8.7	-1.0
Uruguay	1.1	3.4	-4.1	1.6	6.1	4.7	-1.0	-3.3	0.9	1.6	3.6	2.8	1.2	5.3	6.2	6.0	1.9	-9.4
Standard deviation	3.53	1.61	4.61	4.18	2.67	1.79	5.91	6.18	5.36	3.57	3.17	5.34	4.81	6.04	2.49	4.41	6.28	4.41

	1983	1984	1985	1986	1987	1988	1989	1990	1991	1992	1993	1994	1995	1996	1997	1998
Argentina	3.0	2.7	-4.4	7.3	2.6	-1.9	-6.2	0.1	10.0	8.9	5.8	8.3	-3.1	4.4	8.4	4.0
Brazil	-3.4	5.3	7.9	7.5	3.5	-0.1	3.2	-4.4	1.0	-0.5	4.9	5.9	4.2	2.8	3.7	0.2
Paraguay	-3.0	3.1	4.0	0.0	4.3	6.4	5.8	3.1	2.5	1.7	4.0	3.0	4.5	1.1	2.6	0.0
Uruguay	-5.9	-1.1	1.5	8.9	7.9	0.0	1.3	0.9	2.9	7.4	3.1	5.5	-2.0	5.0	5.1	2.5
Standard deviation	3.77	2.66	5.16	4.01	2.32	3.64	5.16	3.15	4.02	4.49	1.16	2.17	4.01	1.75	2.52	1.92

Source: ECLAC.

49

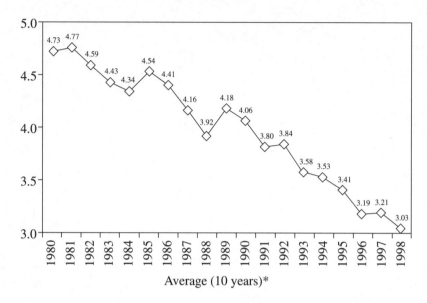

Average (10 years)*

Note: The number for 1980 is the average for 1971–80; the number for 1981 is the average for 1971–80, etc.

Source: Table 3.1.

Figure 3.1   Running mean of the standard deviation of the GDP growth rates of the MERCOSUR countries

standard deviation of the last line of Table 3.1. The numbers in the figure, in each year, refer to ten-year periods ending in the reference year – for example, 1980 should be interpreted as the average of the SD of the last line of Table 3.1, for 1971–80. The figure shows the SD trend between the total growth rates of the four countries. A fall in the indicator means that the GDP growth rates of the four countries tend to differ less between them in the longer term. The graph shows a clear downward trend in the standard deviation. This points to a greater degree of similarity in the behavior of the economies of the region. This trend is reflected in the following elements:

(i)   the average SD between 1989 and 1998 is the lowest in the series under consideration;
(ii)   on the basis of the means of the last line of Table 3.1, for fixed ten-year periods, there is an average fall in the SD of 4.7 in 1971–80, 4.1 in 1981–90 and 2.8 in 1991–98 (eight years in the last);
(iii)   the average SD fell consecutively during the last five observations.

Table 3.2 MERCOSUR inflation (CPI), January/December, 1993–98 (percentages)

Country	1993	1994	1995	1996	1997	1998
Argentina	7.4	3.9	1.6	0.1	0.3	0.9
Brazil	2489.1	929.3	22.0	9.1	4.3	2.5
Paraguay	20.4	18.3	10.5	8.2	6.2	16.0
Uruguay	52.9	44.1	35.4	24.3	15.2	9.4

Note: [a] Provisional.

Source: ECLAC.

In addition, Table 3.2 shows:

(a) in general terms, the trend towards lower inflation in the region, close to international levels;[14] and
(b) fewer differences between the inflation rates of the four countries.

Finally, it is worth noting the similarities in the public debts, measured as a percentage of GDP, of Argentina and Brazil. These two economies are clearly the strongest in the subregion and their public debt, excluding the monetary base, accounts for some 40 per cent of GDP (slightly less in Argentina and slightly more in Brazil). This point is especially important for the implementation of a successful monetary union. If debt levels had been very different *vis-à-vis* GDP, it would have been necessary to generate compensatory primary results in those countries with higher debt levels and, in that case, the taxes introduced with this aim in mind would have hindered the entry of capital and/or prompted capital flight. This would have reduced the internal consistency of policies in the subregion and made it more difficult to administer exchange rate and monetary policies in the monetary union. The similarities in the respective public debt levels of the biggest members of that possible union is, therefore, a positive factor for its success and for its unification.

6. WHAT HAS CHANGED SINCE 1997?

As stated above, the idea of establishing monetary union in MERCOSUR was first mooted in 1997. What has changed since this idea emerged two years ago? Or, to put it differently, has the idea of monetary union really strengthened in the 1997–99 period. In this regard, seven important elements should be taken into account, all of which point towards monetary union:

1. The deterioration in relations within the bloc owing to a series of trade frictions. Curiously, this could be viewed by some skeptics as a clear sign that monetary union is nothing more than a utopia. However, the opposite is true, since the fact that integration has until now been limited to trade has prevented the member countries from adopting commitments associated with greater integration (commitments which invariably imply concessions, choices and sacrifices on the part of the members). This has left room for protectionist lobbies of all types to proliferate. Although the metaphor cannot be sustained academically, it is valid to compare MERCOSUR to a pair of lovers who continue their relationship without committing themselves to marriage. This relationship is marked by minor conflicts. The point comes, therefore, when the only way to put an end to these conflicts is for the couple to commit themselves to deepening the relationship and, consequently, to agree to make compromises that will benefit the union. Similarly, problems such as those that affected the sugar sector in Argentina, or the protests against Brazilian phytosanitary controls, will likely be solved only when the sectors involved realize that these commitments are essential to make progress in more important areas.

2. The devaluation of the real. Sharp fluctuations in the real parities between currencies in one area, within which there is free trade, are obviously a worrying factor that works against intra-subregional trade. It is not a coincidence that after the devaluation of the lira in 1992 some European member states demanded retaliatory measures against goods imported from Italy. Similarly, after the devaluation of the real, Argentine producers made similar demands, such as the introduction of a specific tariff against Brazilian goods, safeguard measures, and the establishment of quotas. Although these measures were temporarily justified, they ran against the spirit of free trade that has marked MERCOSUR since its creation. In the last resort, monetary union is the only decisive way to end these types of problems and risks, as well as to avoid a reverse of all subregion achievements in respect of strictly trade related matters – which is related to point (1) above.

3. The consolidation of the euro. In 1997, Luxembourg was the only country complying, *stricto sensu*, with the Maastricht criteria, as distinct from the fiscal problems that affected the 'patrons' of the euro – France and Germany – and doubts over the introduction of the euro as a fiduciary currency on 1 January 1999. Two years later, the euro was adopted as a fiduciary currency in 11 of the 15 members of the European Union. It is

conceivable that once the euro begins to operate as a physical currency in 2002, the 'eurozone' will be enlarged to include 15 countries – with the inclusion of the United Kingdom, Sweden, Denmark and Greece. Most experts believe that, if the negotiations for the accession of six new members to the European Union – involving those countries in the old Eastern European bloc that made successful transitions to capitalism – are concluded satisfactorily, it is likely that in the next decade the euro will become the currency of an even larger bloc, which could include 21 countries.

4. The change in world perception after the crisis that affected the emerging economies in 1997–99. Until recently many authorities and scholars, especially in the USA, had reservations about European monetary union. In this context, any proposal for monetary union in MERCOSUR, with a much more recent integration history than Europe's, was seen as something that was simply unattainable and not even worth discussing. However, after the crises and devaluations in South-East Asia (1997), Russia (1998) and Brazil (1999), the key idea that there should be fewer currencies – as one of the mechanisms that would help avoid future crises – became increasingly popular in different fora and gained a certain academic respectability. The idea of monetary union in MERCOSUR, therefore, was no longer seen as a simple utopia.

5. The favorable evolution of the situation in Brazil. It is clear that, if the integration process is to be deepened, Brazil must achieve macroeconomic balance. In 1997, there was serious concern about the increasing external and fiscal deficits posted by Brazil until then and in 1998. However, data for 1999 suggest an improvement in the next few years in the relationship between: public sector borrowing requirement/GDP and current account deficit/GDP. This is the result of fiscal adjustment measures, on the one hand, and the devaluation of the real on the other.

6. The fall in subregional inflation. Monetary union will not be possible without harmonizing the inflation rates of the countries in the subregion and, preferably, lowering these to the rates of the industrialized countries. In this respect, inflation was still high at the beginning of 1997, with inflation in Brazil and Paraguay standing at close to 10 per cent in 1996 and above 20 per cent in Uruguay. Two years later the outlook turned more favorable although, strictly speaking, there were reverses in Paraguay and inflation in Brazil rose again in 1999. The fact that the exchange rate in Brazil devalued by 80 per cent, in the peak of the overshooting period, and will probably end 1999 with a devaluation of 45 per cent, with a pass-through of some 0.15, and with consumer inflation of under 7 per cent, clearly shows that stabilization in the country is a stronger phenomenon that at first thought, with inflation likely to fall again in 2000 and possibly reaching

OECD convergence in 2001. At the same time, the success of the Uruguayan government's anti-inflation policy has been notable, with a similar convergence likely to occur in the next few years.

7. The change in the situation in Uruguay and Paraguay. In 1997, if the subregional initiatives in favor of monetary integration had proved successful, it would have been highly likely that this would have consisted of a bilateral initiative between Brazil and Argentina, with the subsequent inclusion of MERCOSUR's smaller members. At that moment, high inflation in Uruguay and doubts over Paraguay's status in the bloc – threatened by the risk of institutional breakdown because of the political conflicts in the country – would have made it difficult for these two countries to join the project. Meanwhile, the fall in the inflation rate in Uruguay and the resolution of the Paraguayan crisis, which culminated in the formation of a coalition government, helped make MERCOSUR a more coherent and homogeneous bloc, both economically and politically.

7.   THE VIABILITY OF MONETARY UNION AS A LONG-TERM PROJECT

The natural objection to the adoption of such an ambitious proposal as the monetary union of a group of countries is based on the view that, in the case of MERCOSUR, the necessary conditions for such a project do not exist – that is, the development of a common market that goes beyond a CET, specifically the coordination of macroeconomic policy and the harmonization of national tax, labor and financial legislation. In short, this objection could be expressed in the idea that 'MERCOSUR cannot achieve in ten years what it took Europe four decades to build'. There are, however, four key arguments to consider:

1. The intellectual idea behind European monetary union was the famous 1970 Werner Report, presented 13 years after the 1957 Treaty of Rome, which gave rise to the European Economic Community. The recommendations of the report, however, were dropped after the 1973 oil shock and, specifically, because of the subsequent rise in inflation. Similarly, although MERCOSUR dates back to 1991, its origin lies in the 1986 bilateral agreements between Brazil and Argentina. Therefore, the view that MERCOSUR is advancing more quickly than the European Union with respect to the unification project is erroneous: the most serious discussion of monetary union took place in 1999, 13 years after these agreements were signed. Coincidentally, this is exactly the same length of time that separated the Treaty of Rome (1957) from the first formal mention of monetary union in the Werner Report.

2. No one views monetary union as a short-term project. All the member states acknowledge that this is not a proposal than can be implemented immediately but one that, after all the stages have been completed, could probably become a reality within 10–15 years.
3. In 10–15 years' time, MERCOSUR will be younger than the European Union, but the historical environment is different. In the 1990s, the world economy underwent a more rapid process of transformation than that experienced from the 1960s until the 1980s, and this trend will probably continue in the coming decade. If Europe had four decades to reach the point at which it is today, within a world that moved more slowly, it is unlikely that MERCOSUR will have the same opportunity without running the risk of missing the train of history.
4. Although monetary union can include Uruguay and Paraguay, it is clear that the main difficulty lies in reconciling the interests of Brazil and Argentina. However, the economic, political and diplomatic engineering required for integrating the economies of only two countries such as Brazil and Argentina, although difficult, is simpler than the integration of the 11 countries that form the 'euro zone', including the latecomers of the 'Club Med'. Taking into account the blocs as a whole and considering the number of countries participating in MERCOSUR (four) and the European Union (15), it is clear that it is easier to reconcile the interests of four members than of 15.

In effect, eventual monetary union, so long as it meets a series of prerequisites, could provide benefits for all the MERCOSUR countries. Independently of this, however, it could have a significant impact on the bloc, specifically on the two largest members.

Monetary union would have four main benefits for the subregion as a whole:

1. The transformation of the subregion into an export platform towards third countries. It is necessary to take up again the original aims that motivated the creation of MERCOSUR. These included transforming the bloc into an export platform, based on a market that guaranteed those companies based in the subregion a scale of production sufficiently large to enable them to enjoy benefits of scale that would allow them to operate at reduced costs. This project was frustrated; MERCOSUR continues to be a marginal exporter in global terms, in part because it is an incomplete market, since exchange rate instability continues to be an economic factor in subregional investment decisions. The creation of a single market worth US$1 trillion, including the four economies of the subregion, would be an extremely important factor in persuading those large

     business groups that wish to meet world demand to invest in the sub-region.

2.   Reduction of risk. A commitment to satisfy minimum prerequisites of macroeconomic stability would contribute, per se, to reducing 'country risk'. As the countries of the bloc each began to assume the same kinds of commitments, investors would begin to view the still negative Latin American 'brand' more positively, thereby reducing MERCOSUR's 'region risk'. Finally, once exchange rate policy was perceived as being managed by an independent subregional central bank, the discretional component associated with political interference in exchange rate policy would disappear. This would, in turn, reduce the subregion's 'exchange rate risk'.

3.   A fall in interest rates, in relation to the above – since the basic interest rate of an economy is affected by external interest rates and by the risk components mentioned above. Once these were overcome the interest rate would fall dramatically over time, coming close to those rates prevalent in the more advanced economies, as a result of lower risks in the subregion.

4.   An increase in new investment. Greater confidence about long-term stability and a reduction in interest rates would serve to promote investment in the subregion by groups that operate on a global scale, which would begin to show greater interest in the subregion. Similarly, the new environment would help stimulate domestic investment.

This last point would be particularly important in the case of Brazil and Argentina, where monetary union would increase their investment potential, since local investors would probably be those that would benefit most from an investment boom in the subregion.

As the main member of MERCOSUR, Brazil would be the natural beneficiary of the political strengthening of the bloc – for example, in negotiations and international fora – that monetary union would imply. Rather than being an isolated voice, without power to impose itself in difficult multilateral external negotiations, it would be the spokesman of a bloc that is increasingly important on the world stage.

On the other hand, monetary union would benefit Argentina by ending the uncertainty over Brazil's exchange rate policy, reducing the impact of the so-called 'Brazil dependency'. Although 30 per cent or more of Argentina's exports will continue to be directed towards Brazil, it would no longer suffer the internal problems associated with a unilateral devaluation by Brazil since, once there is monetary union, bilateral parity would, by definition, remain frozen after the respective national currencies disappear.

8. MONETARY UNION, DOLLARIZATION AND CURRENCY BOARD

It is important to differentiate between the proposal that is being made here – monetary union in MERCOSUR – and the idea of dollarization of the economies of the subregion or the countries of Latin America as a whole that is being discussed in some international circles (Hausmann et al., 1999). In fact, the same logic that is used to advocate monetary union can be used to support the proposal to dollarize the economies of the region. However, the implications are completely different.

Dollarization is not an advisable strategy, since there are five types of problems associated with it. These problems are acknowledged even by its proponents:[15]

1. The difficulty of absorbing real shocks.[16] Monetary union 'freezes' the 'relative parity' within the subregion, but is perfectly consistent with the possibility of modifying the exchange rate of the subregion in case of external shocks, such as those involving prices, interest rates or international liquidity conditions. This is not possible with dollarization. Eichengreen's (1998) particularly rigorous observation, originally presented as a criticism of the idea of a regional currency board, is also applicable *ipsis litteris* to the issue of dollarization,

    > pegging each of the MERCOSUR currencies to a common external numeraire like the US dollar is an extremely indirect way of solving the problem of intra-MERCOSUR exchange-rate variability. *It forecloses not just intra-MERCO-SUR exchange-rate changes as an instrument of adjustment but also, in effect, changes in the exchange rate* vis-à-vis *the rest of the world.* (Eichengreen, 1998, p. 24, emphasis added)

2. The lack of a 'lender of last resort'. There is apparently little possibility of a financial crisis hitting the MERCOSUR countries in the near future. If this were to occur, however, both under the present system of multiple currencies and in the system of monetary union, the monetary authorities could act as a lender of last resort in order to inject liquidity into the system. On the other hand, and given that the MERCOSUR countries do not issue dollars, this would not be possible in the case of dollarization. Although it could be possible in the context of an agreement with the USA, it is unlikely that the US authorities, especially the Federal Reserve, would approve such action.

3. The loss of income from seigniorage – emission of money – and from the interest of international reserves. In a situation in which national currencies are substituted by a foreign one, the concept of international reserves

would become meaningless. These losses, especially those associated with interest based on reserves, would be significant for the countries involved. In this case, an international treaty with the USA could lessen the impact of the problem, through some kind of financial compensation for the countries of the subregion. However, as in the aforementioned case, it is doubtful whether this support, which would be provided by US taxpayers, would be so easily forthcoming.

4. The difficulty of sharing sovereignty, or what Hausmann et al. (1999) refer to as 'governance structure' – that is, the resistance to US institutions being 'absorbed' by other countries or, alternatively, to the USA sharing sovereignty with neighbors that, in its view, are not trustworthy. In concrete terms, it is difficult to imagine the Federal Reserve agreeing to having a director on its board nominated by, for example, one of the MERCOSUR countries.

5. The lack of political support for the proposal. Despite the problems highlighted above, situations may arise where the relationship between a country and the USA is so close that the benefits of creating a monetary union with it are greater than the costs. However, for this to occur, several factors should be taken into account, such as public opinion and the view of political leaders. In this respect, it is reasonable to affirm that the dollarization proposal has been embraced by certain small Central American countries and even in Mexico. The latter has already developed very close ties with the USA, has a vast common border, and has historically been the source of mass labor migration to the USA. Therefore, a significant section of Mexican society has relatives resident in the USA and many Mexicans receive remittances from families that have emigrated there. On the other hand, it is unlikely that the proposal would be embraced by Argentina, much less by Brazil, whose ambitions to become a leader in the region and to differentiate itself from the USA are well known.

In general, it is valid to assert that in Europe the euro has been associated with the creation of new institutions – particularly the European Central Bank – to support a *new* currency. This implies the definition of supranational sovereignty in which all members have a voice and a vote. In the case of the dollarization of one or more Latin American countries, however, these would probably be adhering to the institutions, currency and sovereignty of another country, the USA. Dollarization would, therefore, result in geopolitical circumstances completely different from those in Europe.

Among the various possibilities associated with the adoption of monetary union based on a new currency and dollarization, an alternative has been presented by the former Argentine Economy Minister Domingo Cavallo, who proposed that Argentina and Brazil adhere to a currency board system (Cavallo, 1999). This alternative, however, has not only been criticized on the same grounds as dollarization, but is not supported by Brazil. Regardless, if a single currency is adopted in the subregion and Argentina continues to apply its fixed exchange rate system, it would be necessary to develop a transition mechanism to minimize the likelihood of a speculative attack before defining the conversion rates between one currency and another. A mechanism could be introduced whereby the bilateral peso/real parties would be maintained rigidly during a certain period of time before the two currencies disappeared.

9. A PROPOSAL FOR A WORKING AGENDA

The basic proposition of this study is that the coordination of macroeconomic policy – essential for the viability of monetary union – is necessary to avoid reverses and to promote new advances in the MERCOSUR integration process. It is also vital to prevent the integration process – hereto limited to intra-sub-regional free trade, with a common external tariff – from stagnating. An empirical analysis of MERCOSUR makes it impossible to reject the hypothesis that there is an inverse relationship between the variability of the intra-subregional exchange rate and the intensity of trade flows within MERCOSUR. This hypothesis was apparently confirmed by the recent experience of the devaluation of the Brazilian currency. Consequently, the stabilization of the exchange rate parities between the member states, through greater macroeconomic coordination, could have a positive impact on intra-subregional trade flows (Paiva Abreu and Bevilaqua, 1995). This could eventually lead to monetary union, which is in effect an extreme form of stabilization of these parities.

For such an ambitious proposal to have any chance of success, the MERCOSUR countries obviously need to make considerable progress towards harmonizing their respective national legislation, principally in the areas of tax, labor and capital markets.[17]

However, it is first necessary to define a three-year (2000–2003) working agenda. This would operate on different levels and consist of a time period during which the principal members of MERCOSUR would not be subject to the discontinuities associated with presidential elections. The objective would be to achieve the necessary conditions to be able to sign an agreement in the final year of the present Brazilian government (2002). This agreement would set the final year of the subsequent government (2006) as the deadline for establishing a date for monetary union.[18] At present, the steps required are so many and so large that the definition of dates is still premature; hence the proposal to work towards a position in which these dates can be defined more precisely within a few years.

It is worth noting that 2002 is not being presented as the year in which this process will begin, but rather as the year in which the MERCOSUR countries will commit themselves to define, in 2006, the date of monetary union, which would probably not take place before 2010. In this case, 2006 would represent for MERCOSUR what 1992 represented for European unification – a kind of 'initial sprint' in the race towards unification. However, given that the process involves a small group of countries with certain 'know-how' in currency exchange rates, it may not be necessary to wait ten years between this start-up and the onset of the physical circulation of a new currency, as occurred in Europe – where this stage will only start in 2002, a decade after the Maastricht Treaty. In MERCOSUR, it could happen in a shorter period. A realistic date for introducing a single currency in the subregion would be between 2010 and 2015. If this process is completed near to this latter date, then monetary union would have been achieved three decades after the start of Argentine–Brazilian integration in 1986 – when the seed of MERCOSUR was first sown – a time period that is not much shorter than the four decades in Europe that separated the 1957 Treaty of Rome from the recent adoption of the euro as a fiduciary currency.

Monetary integration would thus include some key dates. The first is 1998, when the MERCOSUR countries, through their presidents, signed the Act of Ushuaia at the 14th meeting of the Common Market Council in which

> the MERCOSUR leaders announced that the process of deepening the customs union should be completed through new measures capable of: (a) defining fiscal and investment disciplines, (b) working towards the harmonization of macroeconomic policies and (c) *considering other aspects that could in the future facilitate the establishment of a single currency in the Southern Common Market.* (Emphasis added)

Although the declaration is ambiguous, it was important in that it was the first explicit, official and joint mention of monetary union as a long-term aim. The second key date is 2002, when this article suggests the countries should formally commit themselves to define before 2006 – the third key date – the date for monetary union, establishing an agenda on the progress that has to be made in the 2003–6 period. A date for unification would be fixed once this agenda was successfully completed.

In the 2000–2002 period specifically, it is suggested that the working agenda focus on three fronts:

1. The unresolved agenda. The long list of strictly trade-related conflicts must be resolved, including those relating to the automobile sector, the inclusion of the sugar sector in the negotiations, and the criteria for phytosanitary controls. The aim would basically be to 'clean up the guidelines' on trade

issues; create a 'pure' free trade area; and avoid 'perforations' in the CET. In this way, the discrepancies in relations within the bloc would be reduced, current differences would be eliminated and the road towards a 'pure' CET would be defined before 2002. Thus, it is expected that the negotiations could make progress beyond mere trade issues from 2003. In this case, in the 2003–6 period, the negotiations would involve the so-called 'new issues', such as consumer rights, fair competition, government procurement, and the concept of 'national treatment', which are complex issues but in certain respects under the jurisdiction of the executive. It would also include legislative harmonization in the three areas already mentioned – tax, labor and capital markets – which would imply greater parliamentary participation in the negotiations.

2. Statistical standardization. The decisions adopted at the 15 June presidential meeting on standardizing the criteria for defining and measuring the main macroeconomic variables in a more homogeneous manner was an important step forward. The aim would be regularly to publish a series of economic indicators that would: (i) make comparisons; and (ii) define a subregional measure for each of these indicators, which lays the foundation of any ambitious integration effort.

3. Macroeconomic coordination.[19] It is proposed that in 2000 the MERCOSUR countries negotiate and approve a 'Protocol of Macroeconomic Coordination', through which they commit themselves to put into practice, by 2002, a 'three 3 per cent ceilings' rule, establishing:[20]

   - a 3 per cent ceiling on inflation;
   - a 3 per cent GDP ceiling on the nominal deficit of the consolidated public sector; and
   - a 3 per cent GDP ceiling on the deficit of the current account of the balance of payments.

It is important to note that these parameters represent, as stated above, ceilings, not goals, since some countries currently register better indicators than these. In other words, the aim is that in around three years the four MERCOSUR countries would: first, have an inflation rate close to international levels; second, respect the same public sector deficit established in Maastricht for the euro countries; and third, have certain modest external disequilibria goals, which is particularly important owing to the crises that affected Mexico in 1994–95, the South-East Asia countries in 1997, and Brazil in 1999. However, nothing will prevent each country from eventually deciding to adopt more or less rigid goals than the aforementioned ceilings.

The benefits of a gradualist strategy, *vis-à-vis* a more rapid integration strategy, are twofold. First, it allows sequential consensuses to be constructed – that is, to establish successive agreements leaving particularly difficult issues to one side, so long as the issue is not of vital importance. A common exchange rate policy is one example. In particular, it is an issue that will have to be discussed in the future but that today is a 'taboo' subject in the negotiations – because of the differences between the exchange rate regimes in Argentina and Brazil, which neither country is willing to abandon – and it makes little sense to discuss it in the current stage of MERCOSUR's development. Second, the strategy is consistent with the respective national agendas – that is, it seeks to define macroeconomic policies that will benefit the integration process but that will also help improve each country's economy.[21] Brazil, for example, will benefit greatly if it succeeds in lowering its fiscal deficit, in the same way that Argentina will benefit if the trend there towards external disequilibria is reversed.

By 2003, therefore, the MERCOSUR economies should become more homogeneous and share what is generically understood as 'macroeconomic equilibrium'. This would allow them to develop into attractive centers for foreign or domestic investment. The risks of speculative attacks against their national currencies should also diminish. In turn, this would induce the countries to speed up the integration process, advancing beyond the progress made thus far. In this context, a new working agenda for the 2003–6 period would be established, and a date for monetary union could finally be defined by 2006.

In this respect, it is worth examining the essential condition for the success of any ambitious integrationist initiative: the political will of governments, which need these initiatives to succeed – despite the fact that the 'ideal' conditions for monetary union are still absent. Otherwise, in the absence of such a will, progress will simply not be made. As Mintz (1970) states,

> It has often been argued that the conditions under which monetary integration might reasonably be expected to succeed are very restrictive. In fact, these conditions appear no more restrictive than the conditions for the establishment of a successful common market. *The major, and perhaps only, real condition for the institution of either is the political will to integrate on the part of prospective members.* (p. 33, emphasis added; quoted in Cohen, 1993, p. 200)

The importance of a gradualist approach is underlined by the latest events that have affected MERCOSUR and, specifically, the bilateral relationship between Brazil and Argentina. In view of the arguments presented here, the answer to the question 'Does monetary union in MERCOSUR make sense?' is 'Yes'. However, the answer to the question 'Is this a viable option in the short term?' is obviously 'No', if one takes into account the long list of unresolved issues that still need to be settled before an official calendar towards monetary union can be defined. An example of the type of problem that needs to be resolved is that of the non-tariff barriers (NTBs) that the MERCOSUR countries have been increasingly introducing since 1996. The NTBs, which numbered 285 when the Protocol of Ouro Preto was signed, reached 350 in 1998.[22] Consequently, completing the free trade zone and the customs union is the first step to be taken if more ambitious integration proposals are to succeed. Once this stage is complete, and once the MERCOSUR economies become increasingly harmonized, with more adjusted and relatively homogeneous macroeconomic indicators, the issue of monetary union will feature more naturally on the agenda, following an evolutionary path very similar to that adopted by Europe over the last 40 years.

NOTES

* This chapter was prepared originally for the Workshop 'Towards Macroeconomic Convergence in MERCOSUR? Lessons from the European Monetary Union', St Antony's College, University of Oxford, 12 June 2001. Therefore, it does not take into account the 2001–2 Argentina crises.
1. Some of the issues discussed here, based on the idea of 'shared sovereignty', were first presented in Araújo (1992), although the issues have not been examined closely.
2. See IPEA (1997) for a strictly commercial analysis of initial developments in MERCOSUR and its prospects.
3. In employing a metaphor used by a diplomat active in the integration process between countries of the region, MERCOSUR's dynamism can be compared to water-skiing, since 'if the boat stops, the skier falls'.
4. See Nofal (1998) for a critique of the proposal.
5. Menem's first reference to the issue, at the end of April 1997, was made soon after his bilateral meeting with his Brazilian counterpart Fernando Henrique Cardoso. In a subsequent press conference, Menem said that 'we should begin to think about a common currency'. This statement was supported by the Brazilian president, who said that 'the moment for a common currency and for the convergence of macroeconomic policy will come' (*Gazeta Mercantil*, 28 April 1997). Subsequently, Argentine Economy Minister Roque Fernández said in a statement made in that country that 'in the future, we are going to focus on integrating the capital and financial markets, which will directly point towards a single currency. If we can commit ourselves to integrate the capital markets, making progress on a single currency will only depend on fiscal coordination in the different countries' (*Gazeta Mercantil*, 29 April 1997).
6. See an article published in 1997 by President Carter's former advisor on National Security Affairs (1977–80) on the USA's geopolitical strategy towards the countries of Eurasia, which examines possible scenarios involving the countries of the former Soviet Union in the 2005–10 period (Brzezinski, 1997, pp. 19–24).
7. See Almeida (1998) for a more detailed examination of the future of MERCOSUR.
8. See Hoekman and Leidy (1993) for an analysis of the origins of and a discussion on some of the problems associated with European integration.
9. The Single European Act of 1986 represented a commitment of the countries of the European Economic Community to create a common market totally free of barriers to the free circulation of goods, capital and labor within the member states of the agreement by the end of 1992.
10. Apart from the general questions examined in this section, a process of unification implies resolving a series of operational issues relating to, among other things, the way in which

financial markets operate. See McCauley and White (1997) for a detailed analysis of the European case. See Begg (1997) for an examination of the specific issues of monetary policy in a process of unification between national currencies, also with reference to the European case.

11. See Masson and Taylor (1992) for a survey of this literature, especially section III of these authors' study.
12. These three points, points (1) to (3), are based in part on Schweickert, Zahler and Jessen (1997).
13. The last line therefore corresponds to the standard deviation of the four values presented in each column.
14. This trend will be negatively affected in 1999 by a rise in inflation in Brazil, the result of the devaluation of the real. However, the trend is likely to resume in 2000. In the case of Argentina, the modest increase is simply the consequence of natural fluctuations in the CPI variation, when this fell sharply to nearly zero.
15. See Larraín (1999) for a balanced critique of the dollarization proposal.
16. Some of the critical comments made against the dollarization thesis are also applicable to the currency board system. However, given the limits of this chapter, it is not possible to make any comments on the validity of such a system in the case of Argentina. What concerns us is simply to defend the arguments in favor of monetary union *vis-à-vis* the arguments in favor of dollarization.
17. In respect of tax harmonization, for example, see González Cano (1996), Gandra (1997) and Gómez Sabaini (1999). For an excellent but relatively skeptical analysis of the lack of financial integration in MERCOSUR see Paiva Abreu (1997).
18. The importance of Brazil's political calendar lies in the fact that, since the country is obviously the key to the success of the negotiations, it is vital that the terms of what is agreed are extensively discussed by its authorities in the years before their conclusion so that any final decision does not have to be taken by a recently elected government that has not participated in previous debates. This strategy is also relevant in the case of Argentina, whose president takes office in December, at the end of the first year of his counterpart in Brazil, where the presidential mandate begins in January.
19. See Strauss-Kahn (1997) for a discussion on the different alternatives for coordination.
20. This focus is consistent with the caution that has characterized the initial negotiations in the bloc on the proposal for monetary union. This caution was highlighted by Brazilian President Fernando Henrique Cardoso when he said: 'Without fiscal responsibility healthy integration cannot be achieved. A common currency will never be introduced without very serious prior efforts which economists call fundamental . . . Without solid fundamentals, the single currency [is] an illusion' (*Jornal do Brasil*, 16 June 1999).
21. At the same time, it is assumed that each country makes important progress in its respective reform agenda, but could contribute towards greater harmonization of the respective macroeconomic situations and legislation, such as tax reform in Brazil; reform of the labor market in Argentina; or the ongoing policies towards gradually reducing inflation in Uruguay.
22. The figure is from Felipe de la Balze.

REFERENCES

Almeida, Paulo Roberto de (1998), 'Brasil y el futuro del MERCOSUR: dilemas y opciones', *Integration & Trade*, **6** (September–December), Buenos Aires: IDB/Intal, pp. 65–82.
Araújo, José Tavares Jr. (1992), 'A opção por soberanias compartidas na América Latina: o papel da economia brasileira', *Revista de Economía Política*, **12** (1), pp. 90–106.
Begg, David (1997), *The design of EMU*, IMF Working Paper, WP/97/99.

Bovenberg, A. et al. (1991), 'Economic and Monetary Union in Europe and Constraints on National Budgetary Policies', *IMF Staff Papers*, **38** (2).

Brzezinski, Zbigniew (1997), 'Uma geoestratégia para a Eurásia', *Foreign Affairs*, reproduced in *Gazeta Mercantil*, 12 September.

Cavallo, Domingo (1999), 'Brasil: Remedios Caseros o Buena Medicina', *Archivos del Presente*, Year 4, n. 15 (January–March), Buenos Aires.

Cohen, Benjamin (1993), 'Beyond EMU: the Problem of Sustainability', *Economics and Politics*, **5** (2), pp. 187–204.

Collignon, Stefan, Bofinger, Peter, Johnson, Christopher and De Maigret, Bertrand (1994), *Europe's Monetary Future*, NJ: Rutherford, NJ: Fairleigh Dickinson University Press.

Delors, Jacques (1997), 'Keep on keeping on', *Newsweek*, 3 February.

Eichengreen, Barry (1998), *'Does MERCOSUR Need a Single Currency?'*, paper presented at the conference Alca and MERCOSUR: the Brazilian Economy and the Process of Subregional and Hemispheric Integration, Brasília, 5 and 6 October.

Eichengreen, Barry (1997), 'Free trade and macroeconomic policy', paper presented at World Bank's Annual Latin American Conference on Research on Development Economics, Montevideo, 30 June and 1 July.

Eichengreen, Barry (1993), 'European Monetary Unification', *Journal of Economic Literature*, **31** (September), pp. 1321–57.

Englander, S. and Egebo, T. (1993), 'Adjustments under Fixed Exchange Rates: Application to the European Monetary Union', *OECD Economic Studies*, **20**.

European Community Commission (ECC) (1990), 'One Market, One Money', *European Economy*, **44** (October).

Gandra, Ives (1997), 'Tributação no MERCOSUL', *Conjuntura Econômica*, April, pp. 21–7.

Giambiagi, Fabio (1997), 'Una proposta de unificação monetária dos países do MERCOSUL', *Revista de Economia Política*, **17**(4) (October–December), pp. 5–30.

Giambiagi, Fabio (1998), 'Moeda única no MERCOSUL: notas para o debate', *Revista Brasileira de PolÌtica Internacional: Notas para o Debate*, Year 41, n. 1, pp. 24–38.

Giavazzi, Francesco and Giovannini, Alberto (1991), *Limiting Exchange Rate Flexibility – The European Monetary System*, 3rd edn, Cambridge, MA: The MIT Press.

Giavazzi, Francesco and Pagano, Marco (1988), 'The Advantage of Tying One's Hands: EMS Discipline and Central Bank Credibility', *European Economic Review*, **32**, pp. 1055–75.

Gómez Sabaini (1999), 'Política impositiva común: la visión argentina y brasileña', paper presented at the seminar Brazil–Argentina. Instituto de Pesquisa de Relações Internacionais (IPRI), Fundação Alexandre de Gusmão. Río de Janeiro, 10 and 11 June.

González Cano, Hugo (1996), *Armonización Tributaria del MERCOSUR*, Buenos Aires: Ediciones Académicas.

Hausmann, Ricardo et al. (1999), 'Financial Turmoil and the Choice of Exchange Rate Regime', Inter-American Development Bank (IDB).

Hoekman, Bernard and Leidy, Michael (1993), 'Holes and loopholes in integration agreements: history and prospects', in Anderson, Kym and Blackhurts, *Regional Integration and the Global Trading System*, New York: St Martin's Press, ch. 10, pp. 218–45.

IPEA (1997), 'O mercado regional: expansão e perspectivas do MERCOSUL', in IPEA, *O Brasil na virada do milênio*, Rio de Janeiro, ch. II. 3, pp. 153–65.

Larraín, Felipe (1999), 'Going green', *Worldlink*, May–June, pp. 38–40.

Lavagna, Roberto (1996), 'MERCOSUR: Consistencia densa o leve?', paper presented at the seminar MERCOSUR e a Integração Sul-americana: mais do que economia, Fortaleza, 13–18 December.

Lavagna, Roberto and Giambiagi, Fabio (1998), 'MERCOSUR: hacia la creación de una moneda común', *Archivos del Presente*, Year 3, n. 12, April–June, pp. 45–62.

Masson, Paul and Taylor, Mark (1992), 'Issues in the operation of monetary unions and common currency areas', in Goldstein, Morris, Isard, Peter, Masson, Paul and Taylor, Mark (eds), *Policy Issues in the Evolving International Monetary System* (Occasional Paper 96), Washington, DC: IMF, June.

McCauley, Robert and White, William (1997), 'The Euro and European Financial Markets', (Working Paper n. 41), Bank for International Settlements (BIS).

Mintz, Norman (1970) 'Monetary Union and Economic Integration', New York University Graduate School of Business Administration.

Nofal, Beatriz (1998), 'Moneda común en el MERCOSUR: Propuesta aconsejable, factible o distracción?', paper presented at the seminar Coordinación de políticas macroeconómicas en el MERCOSUR. Hacia una moneda única, Fundación Gobierno y Sociedad, Buenos Aires, 12 and 13 June.

Paiva Abreu, Marcelo de (1997), 'Integración Financiera en los países del MERCO-SUR', *Integración & Trade*, n. 1. (January–April), Buenos Aires: IDB/Intal.

Paiva Abreu, Marcelo de and Bevilaqua, Alfonso (1995), 'Macroeconomic Coordination and Economic Integration: Lessons for a Western Hemisphere Free Trade Area', Discussion Text, 340, Rio de Janeiro, November.

Rigolon, Francisco and Giambiagi, Fabio (1999), 'Áreas monetárias ótimas: teoria, unificação monetária européia e aplicações para o MERCOSUL', *Economía Aplicada*, **3**(1) (January–March), pp. 79–108.

Sandholtz, Wayne (1993), 'Choosing union: monetary politics and Maastricht', *International Organization*, **47** (1).

Schweickert, Rainer, Zahler, Roberto and Jessen, Anneke (1997), 'European Economic and Monetary Union: Recent Progress and Possible Implications for Latin America and the Caribbean', paper presented at the seminar Single Currency of the European Union–Euro, on the occasion of the Annual Meeting of Bank Governors–IDB, Barcelona, Spain, 18 March.

Strauss-Kahn, Marc (1997), 'Coordinación monetaria y el papel de los Bancos Centrales: Por qué?, Cuando?, y Cómo?, paper presented at the seminar Armonización bancaria, liberalización financiera y movimientos de capitales en el marco de un área integrada, final document. Centro de Formación para la Integración Regional (CEFIR). Montevideo, 6–8 October.

4. Macroeconomic coordination in MERCOSUR – a sceptical view[1]

Arturo O'Connell

1. INTRODUCTION

At first sight there should be very little doubt that MERCOSUR has been an engine of growth, not only for its member countries, but for the world as a whole, since its imports from outside the region have been growing much faster than world trade.[2]

However, a more detailed examination reveals several weaknesses concerning the performance of MERCOSUR. Some of these are generic, since they affect the Latin American region as a whole. Others are specific and show some degree of failure in achieving the goals for which it was set up.

As to the general weaknesses, MERCOSUR suffers from the same problems that affected most of the Latin American economies during the 1990s; that is, although exports have been increasing at a faster pace than in previous decades, imports increased even faster.[3] Consequently, high balance of trade deficits have prevailed, giving way to even worse current account deficits.[4] Persistent current account deficits, although to a great extent financed by foreign direct investment, have led to a soaring foreign indebtedness, the service of which – besides the continuous trade deficits and the remittance of profits by foreign companies – has made those deficits worsen progressively.[5] As a result, most countries have placed themselves in a position in which new foreign funds are annually required just to cover their deficits. Such a situation makes them vulnerable to shifts of mood in the international financial market, which might also be explained by their worsening debt ratios.

If compared with Mexico, for instance, the specific fact about MERCO-SUR is that even while intra-MERCOSUR trade has shown a significant rise in the exchange of manufactured products – some of them with advanced technical content – extra-MERCOSUR trade is still characterized by domination of primary products or the export of traditional manufactured products.[6] In fact, MERCOSUR shows an almost complete absence of world-class competitors, with the exception of some traditional manufactures (for instance, soybean oil in the case of Argentina, wood pulp and paper products in the case of Brazil). Hopes of being able to join world trade flows at another level, through economies of scale and the experience of competition within a broad, but still restricted market, have not yet materialized.

In order for MERCOSUR countries to begin a new phase of sustainable development they must overcome both their specific and generic weaknesses regarding their pattern of trade as well as their external relationships with the world at large. A certain degree of autonomy in pursuing their policy goals can only be achieved in this way. So the question becomes: what kind of policies would be needed to overcome what could be seen as the obstacles in the road to further development of MERCOSUR?

The scene has been complicated by public disagreements between high-ranking officials of several MERCOSUR countries who have been openly criticizing other member countries and their authorities. The causes of most of these disagreements can be found in a series of partial conflicts at the sectoral level. Such conflicts, though few in number, are enough – following a classical pattern of forceful lobbying – to spread an atmosphere of gloom about the general achievements of MERCOSUR.

The decline in intra-MERCOSUR trade that took place after the Brazilian devaluation – which affected several companies and sectors that had made considerable profits during the previous boom – has only added another generic argument to those partial conflicts at the sectoral level. But we should remember that intra-trade levels within all the Latin American regional agreements – not only in the case of MERCOSUR – had plunged deeper than foreign trade in general during that particular year. The explanation is quite clear and has to do with the aforementioned fact: intra-regional trade tends to show a larger participation of income-elastic goods than those traditionally predominant in external trade agreements. Therefore, every time international market events have resulted in a recession during the last few years – either in terms of trade slumps or reduced financial inflows – trade within the regional agreements framework has, in turn, tended to decline more than proportionately.

Thus the obstacles to the consolidation and further progress of MERCOSUR are much more the result of microeconomic issues than macroeconomic ones concerning relative exchange rates or coordination of fiscal and/or monetary policies. It is a matter of some sectors whose lack of present-day competitiveness – so-called 'trade-sensitive' sectors – would demand specific policies of adjustment to a higher degree of trade 'openness'. This need for adjustment, incidentally, originates in competition, not only from MERCOSUR member countries but from the rest of the world as well. Therefore, it will not be sorted out by applying intra-regional limitations on imports. But going beyond a defensive attitude, it is also a matter of developing an industrial structure capable of gaining a larger share in the world markets.

However, many MERCOSUR country observers and authorities have pinned all their hopes of overcoming the pains of growth that integration involves on achieving some kind of macroeconomic coordination that would eventually lead to a common currency. Therefore, this chapter is devoted to studying the merits of the argument in favour of such a solution to present-day problems.

2. THE DEGREE OF 'REAL' INTEGRATION OF MERCOSUR ECONOMIES

A possible justification for the importance of macroeconomic coordination – as pertaining to the 'real' side of the economies – revolves around the 'optimal currency area' (OCA) kind of argument, of which there are several. Let us examine them one by one.

2.1 Reciprocal Opening among MERCOSUR Countries

The first argument derived from an OCA viewpoint has to do with the degree of integration achieved or about to be achieved in the near future among the member countries.

In spite of a determined application of policies aimed at opening up each of the two major countries and the implementation of an intra-MERCOSUR trade liberalization, both Argentina's and Brazil's economies remain tightly closed. And even if a much higher proportion of their foreign trade is now covered by the customs union, it is still a far cry from, for instance, EU proportions. The same consideration applies, to some extent, to the other two member countries. As may be gauged from Tables 4.1 and 4.2, even after

Table 4.1   MERCOSUR: foreign trade opening to the world and to MERCOSUR (1998)

	Trade/GDP (%)	Intra-MERCOSUR Trade/total trade (%)	Intra-trade/ GDP (%)
Argentina	8.9	36.2	3.2
Brazil	6.6	17.1	1.1
Paraguay	9.3	60.9	5.7
Uruguay	12.4	49.7	6.1

Sources: International trade figures from WTO Web_pube.zip; GDP figures from IMF, WEO Database, April 2000. Intra-MERCOSUR trade vs aggregate foreign trade, figures derived from CEI, *Informe MERCOSUR*, Buenos Aires, July 1999.

Table 4.2   European Union: exports, total and intraEU, and GDP (2000)

	GDP (US$ billion)	Total Exports (US$ billion)	Total Exports GDP (%)	IntraEU exports/ Total exports (%)	IntraEU exports/ GDP (%)
Austria	188.7	64.3	34.1	61.4	20.9
Belgium	228.8	187.8	82.1	74.9	61.5
Denmark	162.7	53.8	33.1	67.3	22.2
Finland	121.3	44.5	36.7	55.3	20.3
France	1294.2	298.8	23.1	61.3	14.2
Germany	1866.2	549.6	29.4	56.5	16.6
Greece	112.6	10.7	9.5	43.6	4.2
Ireland	95.3	76.8	80.6	60.0	48.3
Italy	1074.0	238.3	22.2	54.9	12.2
Luxembourg	18.9	7.8	41.3	84.0	34.7
Netherlands	369.5	208.3	56.4	78.8	44.4
Portugal	106.2	23.3	22.0	79.5	17.4
Spain	560.9	113.3	20.2	68.5	13.8
Sweden	229.0	86.9	37.9	55.0	20.9
United Kingdom	1427.4	281.6	19.7	56.9	11.2
EU-15 countries	7855.9	2246.0	28.6	62.1	17.8

Source: UNCTAD Handbook of Statistics On-line, 2002 edition, Tables 7.1 for GDP figures, 1.1 for Total Export Values and 3.1 and 4.1. for Trade Structure by Destination.

nearly a decade of economic integration and opening up, commercial interdependence among all MERCOSUR countries has proven to be slight if compared to that achieved by EU countries, currently undergoing a process of monetary unification.

Geography – under the wholesale trade liberalization process that MERCOSUR countries have been going through – plus regional preference should contribute to further interdependence in the future. A much closer examination of the evolution of intra-MERCOSUR exports and imports, however, shows a significant asymmetry.

According to Table 4.3, the share of other members in total exports has more than doubled for MERCOSUR countries as a whole, if compared with the situation at the beginning of the integration process. But the share of MERCOSUR in total imports has increased only slightly. Individually speaking, it could be shown that the increase has only been significant in the case of Paraguay.

Table 4.3   MERCOSUR: share of MERCOSUR in exports and imports, 1990–99 (in percentages)

	1990	1991	1992	1993	1994	1995	1996	1997	1998	1999
Share of exports	8.9	11.1	14.3	18.5	19.2	20.4	22.7	24.4	25.0	20.4
Share of imports	14.5	15.3	18.4	19.6	19.2	18.7	20.5	20.9	21.4	19.3

Source: BID, Integración y Comercio en América, Nota Periódica Diciembre de 2000, Anexo Estadistico, Cuadro 7.

Obviously, the explanation for such an asymmetry is that MERCOSUR imports have increased at a much faster pace than exports, a widespread and previously mentioned characteristic of Latin American development during the 1990s.

Therefore, trade interdependence will not necessarily progress at a fast pace when, as a consequence of external financial pressures, the imports of member countries might be expanding slowly, if not declining, as in the case of Argentina, which is mired in a lengthy recession.

2.2   The Different Foreign Trade Composition among MERCOSUR Countries

Besides the small intra-MERCOSUR dependence in terms of trade, the external trade composition of MERCOSUR countries varies widely, as shown in Tables 4.4 and 4.5.

To begin with, the share of manufactured products in exports seems to be quite different between the two major countries. And in the case of Uruguay,

Table 4.4   MERCOSUR: exports by product categories, 1999

	Argentina (%)	Brazil (%)	Paraguay (%)	Uruguay (%)
Primary products	31.6	18.3	55.1	16.4
Agricultural	21.2	11.7	55.1	16.2
Mining	2.4	6.6	0.0	0.2
Energy	8.0	0.0	–	–
Manufactured products	67.1	80.0	44.9	83.4
Traditional	27.9	29.7	35.7	66.2
Food, beverages and tobacco	19.8	16.2	17.8	38.5
Other traditional	8.0	13.5	17.9	27.7
Economies of scale	24.9	24.7	7.8	8.5
Durables	7.4	8.4	0.3	5.5
Technical progress disseminators	6.8	17.2	1.1	3.2
Other goods	1.3	1.7	0.0	0.2
Total	100.0	100.0	100.0	100.0

Source: CEPAL (2001).

Table 4.5   MERCOSUR: imports by product categories, 1999

	Argentina (%)	Brazil (%)	Paraguay (%)	Uruguay (%)
Primary products	3.8	13.4	5.2	11.3
Agricultural	2.3	5.6	3.6	4.4
Mining	0.7	1.0	0.2	0.4
Energy	0.8	6.8	1.4	6.5
Manufactured products	95.2	86.6	94.8	87.9
Traditional	18.0	10.3	27.1	25.7
Food, beverages and tobacco	3.2	3.1	13.5	7.2
Other traditional	14.8	7.2	13.6	18.5
Economies of scale	23.8	26.2	24.3	24.1
Durables	14.1	8.2	15.0	11.6
Technical progress disseminators	39.3	41.9	28.3	26.5
Other goods	1.0	0.0	0.0	0.8
Total	100.0	100.0	100.0	100.0

Source: CEPAL (2001).

whose overall share of manufactures is close to that of Brazil, its more detailed composition once again proves to be different, as it is dominated by 'traditional' products (food, beverages and tobacco, plus textiles and footwear). Machinery, pharmaceutical products and instruments – the so-called 'technical progress disseminators' – appear in a significant proportion only in Brazilian exports. A considerable difference can be found even among the primary products; that is, Argentina is the only fuel exporter while Brazil is the only country strong in mining exports.

The composition of imports to some extent mirrors the above composition of exports. Argentina is significantly self-sufficient in primary products while Brazil is an importer of certain food products – wheat, for instance – as well as oil, both of which are prone to considerable price volatility.[7]

Therefore, 'real' shocks stemming from the world economy are, in principle, quite different for each country. In fact, for the two major members of MERCOSUR, shocks in cereal and oil prices play a totally opposite role.

Asymmetries are thus rampant. But on the other hand, it might be assumed that those almost opposing shocks could bring about certain forms of regional compensation.

Regional transfers, however, can hardly be envisaged. As may be seen from Table 4.6, there is an enormous difference in size between the different countries. Additionally – and in contrast with the EU case – the undeniably largest country is not – at least in terms of per capita income – the wealthiest one. In 1998, Brazil represented 81 and 72 per cent, respectively, in terms of population and area of the whole of MERCOSUR, as well as 68 per cent of its GDP. But its per capita income – at purchasing parity exchange rates – was then 37 per cent lower than the average for the whole of the customs union area.

Table 4.6   MERCOSUR: basic data, 1998

	Population (000s)	Area (km^2)	GDP (US$ billion)	Exports (US$ billion)	GDP–PPP per head (in US$)
World	5 923 083	135 586 199	29 255.9	5 434.0	6 870
South America	331 889	17 818 698	1 503.4	136.2	6 620
MERCOSUR	205 042	11 863 018	1 148.6	81.4	7 762
Argentina	36 123	2 766 889	339.8	26.4	11 940
Brazil	165 158	8 511 969	776.9	51.1	6 840
Paraguay	5 220	406 750	10.9	1.0	4 380
Uruguay	3 239	177 410	21.0	2.8	8 750

Sources: UNCTAD, *Handbook of International Trade and Development Statistics*, 2000 and the World Bank, *World Development Indicators*, 2001. For PPP income per head and for exports, *World Merchandise Trade by region and selected economy*, prepared by Merchandise Trade Section, Statistics Division, WTO, March 2000.

Under such conditions, transfers that might be necessary in order to compensate for the different development levels and/or for differential external shocks – although justifiable in their own terms and potentially wealth-enhancing for everybody involved – sound, in practical terms, almost implausible.[8] In fact, there has been no provision for such transfers in MERCOSUR policies, even in the case of the two smaller countries.[9]

2.3   Labour Flows inside MERCOSUR

Another of the preoccupations of the literature on OCAs, that is, the liberalization of labour flows – although one of the objectives encompassed by the Treaty of Asunción – has hardly made any progress.[10] As to the labour market flexibility that could accommodate the various asymmetric shocks without migration, Argentina is about on a par with Euroland; that is, it is not particularly flexible.[11] Obviously, the economic restructuring plus recession taking place during the last few years has brought Argentina a '*de facto*' much higher degree of labour market flexibility than that which first meets the eye.

Summing up our review of OCA criteria regarding the 'real' side, therefore, only a weak argument can be made for macroeconomic coordination, let alone for a currency union among MERCOSUR countries.

3.   SYMMETRIES AND ASYMMETRIES IN THE FINANCIAL SPHERE

Recently, however, the literature has also turned its attention to the financial field, looking for reasons that would justify macroeconomic coordination or a common currency.

In the case of MERCOSUR countries, direct financial linkages are almost entirely absent. External financial flows, in every case, stem from and mainly end up in institutions based in the industrialized countries. But some symmetry does arise as a consequence of global financial shocks, as shown in Figure 4.1 below, which illustrates the country risk spread behaviour for both Argentina and Brazil. Though largely congruent, a stronger impact of the 'tequila' effect may be detected in the case of Argentina, while the effects of the 'vodka' shock were worse in the case of Brazil.

Furthermore, differences in both the impact and the posture of economic policy have resulted in different exchange rate changes, as illustrated in Figure 4.2.

Throughout the decade, and even under the enormous pressure unleashed by the 'tequila' effect, Argentina – up to the end of 2001 – did not abandon its commitment to a fixed exchange rate by means of a 'corner' alternative in

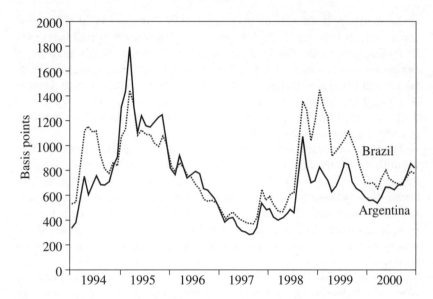

*Figure 4.1   Country risk spread behavior of Argentina and Brazil,
1994–2000*

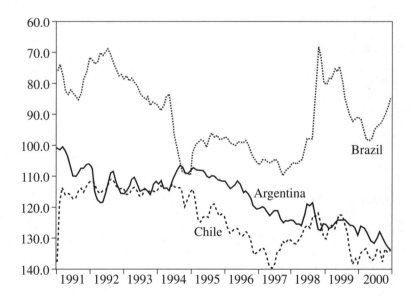

*Figure 4.2   Real broad effective exchange rate indices for Argentina, Brazil
and Chile, 1991–2001 (1990 = 100)*

exchange rate policies, namely the currency board system. As far as Brazil is concerned, its policies changed several times. During the period before the Real Plan, fixed – but periodically changeable – exchange rates were applied. During the first few months of that Plan a commitment to a ceiling was made, which resulted in a significant overvaluation of the new currency. Beginning in March 1995, movable bands – a narrow and a wider one – were used. And from January 1999 onwards the Real was allowed to float, with inflation targeting as the anchor for monetary policy.

Therefore, the conclusion might be drawn that capital flows – whose volatility is related to forces outside the region – do nevertheless have an impact on exchange rates. Also, because this impact is not 'symmetric', or otherwise provoking differential responses from the various players, it results in some intra-MERCOSUR disturbances in terms of exchange rate parities.

In fact, Figure 4.3 shows that such a differential impact has occurred and that, as a result, exchange rate parities have shifted quite significantly over the decade.

Therefore, in the same way as for the 'real' side, on the financial side there is not much justification for macroeconomic coordination or for monetary unification. 'Asymmetries' are found all over.

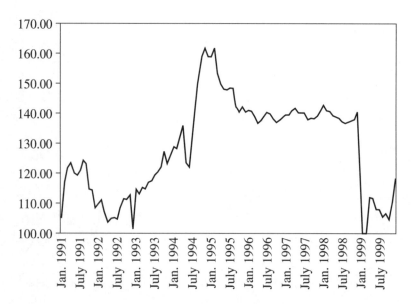

*Figure 4.3   Real exchange rate parity (producer's prices deflated),
          Argentina/Brazil, 1991–99 (1986 = 100)*

Additionally, volatility, in terms of relative exchange rates, does not necessarily lead to serious impacts on trade flows – as was often publicly surmised, particularly in Argentina, against all the evidence – after the devaluation of the real. As already discussed, after all, asymmetries do not seem to matter that much due to the still low degree of reciprocal 'real' integration of MERCOSUR countries.

The general literature on the consequences of exchange rate instability is quite inconclusive. Even the European Union Commission, when arguing over the case for a currency union, could not come up with a larger estimate than a positive 1 per cent impact on the income of its members.

Additionally, in the case of the MERCOSUR countries, the reduced openness of their economies might contribute to an even smaller impact of exchange rate changes on their performance. More specifically, two studies on the determinants of trade flows between Argentina and Brazil have shown a large response to changes in levels of activity in the destination country and a very small one in response to changes in exchange rates.[12]

A detailed study of intra-MERCOSUR trade performance after the 1999 Brazilian devaluation once again confirms that the impact of a relative price change is less than was feared. The recession affecting the various countries has contributed to a decline in foreign trade. And – as has already happened in other cases of Latin American integration areas – intra-regional trade has fallen more than trade as a whole.[13] In the case of the two major countries, more than 61 per cent of the fall in bilateral trade took place exclusively in the motor vehicle industry.[14] A significant plunge in other traditional exports can be observed only in the case of Uruguayan exports to Brazil, but only in commodities such as rice and beef, which are easily saleable in other markets.[15]

The experience of the year 2000 (and even of the first half of 2001), when Argentine exports to Brazil went up 22.9 and 1.5 per cent respectively – in the face of a renewed devaluation of the real – confirms the evidence about the dominance of income factors and the reduced impact of exchange rate changes on trade flows among members.[16]

Therefore, even in this less 'asymmetric' area of external financial shocks, which have resulted in a wide volatility of relative exchange rates in MERCOSUR countries, no serious material damage – in contrast with what is often perceived – has derived neither from it nor from the lack of coordination of their policies.

However, it is also true that if the process of integration and opening up were to follow its course, some increased interaction could arise in the long run. Increasing proportions of tradable goods could be exchanged thus broadening the reciprocal impact of each country's economic performance on the rest. At that point, but not before, macroeconomic coordination might have achieved the relevance that is presently absent.[17]

Having surveyed the effective need for macroeconomic policy coordination, we now turn our attention to its conditions and meaning within the context of the circumstances currently affecting the economies of MERCOSUR.

4. MACROECONOMIC POLICY AND ITS CO-ORDINATION IN MERCOSUR COUNTRIES

First, we examine the limitations of macroeconomic policy in the context of the economies of MERCOSUR and second, we analyse the meaning and potential content of coordination.

4.1   The Limits of Macroeconomic Policy in MERCOSUR Countries

As mentioned before, these economies show very high current account deficits and external debt ratios. New financing is continuously needed in order to pay for imports as well as honor obligations. Under such circumstances – and with an extremely shallow domestic financial market – the degree of macroeconomic policy autonomy is decidedly small.

The 'classical tri-lemma' that forces each and every country to choose only two of these three options: (i) to run an autonomous monetary policy; (ii) to make capital movements free; and (iii) to fix the exchange rate, continues to be repeated with a vengeance.

But additionally, whatever the willingness of the authorities, very little degree of autonomy is left for any monetary policy, no matter what regime is chosen for the exchange rate. And as far as controls on capital movements are concerned, they sound less than credible with modern technology, which is presently coupled with growing administrative decline and, quite frequently, with 'capturing' controllers via the interested private agents. At best some 'friction' might be introduced into these two areas.

With regard to fiscal policy, all the economies of MERCOSUR are fighting a rearguard action to prevent deficits from exploding as a result of the same sort of pressures already experienced by each of the countries involved, as well as additional ones resulting from drastic restructuring and the financial crises. There is almost no room for manoeuvre, since the 'markets' – as well as the IMF – are always breathing down the finance secretaries' necks in order to see that they comply with fiscal consolidation programmes.

Therefore, the whole argument about macroeconomic policy coordination is far from what is potentially feasible in the EU case. In fact, there is very little economic policy making to coordinate.

Moreover, according to the global character of the financial shocks, crisis prevention mechanisms should be set up at this level, rather than at the regional one. Furthermore, and in contrast with what happens in world terms, there is no necessary match between deficits and surpluses at the MERCO-SUR level; that is, each and every member country might simultaneously run a deficit so that no country would be generating a surplus that could be transferred to those other members in more precarious circumstances. It is in this sense that the permanent implicit attempt of Argentina regarding its 'right' to claim a trade surplus with Brazil has only succeeded in bringing a far-reaching conflict into the union.

4.2 Different Degrees and Meanings of Macroeconomic Coordination

Once the circumstances have been considered, the remaining crucial question about macroeconomic coordination in MERCOSUR is whether or not – and to what extent – it would become a driving force to enhance autonomy in the economic policy-making field if compared with that of isolated countries. However, a prior clarification as to what is meant by macroeconomic coordination would be necessary in order to be able to answer this question.

The weakest possible version of such coordination is that of merely an exchange of information about the behaviour of certain macroeconomic variables and at best some corresponding targets for those same variables. But nowadays, each and every member country is carrying out an IMF programme. Additionally, due to the promotion of transparency and standards by the international financial community, such information – and targets for quite a few variables – is available for anyone with access to the Internet and the IMF site. There seems to be very little reason for setting up a specific subregional mechanism unless the information provided to the IMF proved to be distorted and the member countries intended to be more honest with their partners.

A more ambitious second version would envisage a 'peer pressure' mechanism of several degrees relating to the actual fulfilment of those targets. Once again the IMF is in a much better position to achieve this because its loans can be withdrawn at any time, while peers do not seem to have access to any leverage over each other.

A more straightforward third version of coordination would be to adopt certain exchange rate bands among members, coupled with various compensatory mechanisms in case of non-compliance. However, the opportunity and the level of exchange rate parities at which such a mechanism might be introduced could become a serious bone of contention. Back in 1999, for instance, Argentina floated the idea of such a compensatory mechanism against the devaluation of the Real which had taken place in January that same year.

Obviously, Argentina did so without even mentioning the idea of disbursing any compensation for the previous favourable phase, when the Real was undergoing a serious overvaluation. Thus, agreement would be difficult to achieve and, additionally, compensation through trade barriers in a context of high exchange rate volatility would introduce chaos into commercial policy.

A more decisive fourth view of macroeconomic policy coordination would entail an orchestrated joint action in order to respond to various shocks. But, in these most ambitious versions, agreements concerning ends and means – less explicit in the other, milder versions – become unavoidable.

With regard to ends, the exclusive concentration on 'stability' – that is, stability of prices *cum* reduced fiscal deficits *cum* a solid financial system – would have to be subjected to an argument about some basic opinions. As in the case of the EU, most probably a considerable part of the discussion about macroeconomic policy coordination would be dominated by those who believe that 'stability' (in that restricted sense) would either automatically bring along growth and employment or at least that certain trade-offs between that 'stability' and these other goals of policy making could be dismissed. If that were the case, macroeconomic policy coordination could easily be inter-preted only as a thin fig leaf pruriently covering an unlimited advocacy of deflationary policies almost as a permanent regime.

It would also be necessary to take the means issue into consideration: for instance, it is too frequently said that the independence of a central bank is the only guarantee of a serious monetary policy. Is this really so? And would all members agree in granting some regional body total autonomy over this area of policy making?

But, beyond this, and more importantly, a common exchange rate policy will be less than easy to achieve bearing in mind that until very recently totally opposed systems were being followed by the major countries.

Therefore, would macroeconomic coordination be the decisive factor in order to achieve a higher – or a less low – degree of policy autonomy?

Far from it. It could easily become either an innocuous and superfluous exercise aimed at exchanging information about macroeconomic variables and setting up targets without leverage in order to force their compliance, or an attempt at implementing a restrictive 'monetarist' macroeconomic policy at the MERCOSUR level that could result in a vicious cycle of fiscal retrench-ment and recession. It also could easily lead to serious conflicts among member countries in addition to those arising from partial issues at sectoral level.

Consequently, the best that can be said about macroeconomic policy coor-dination is that it would become a *fuite an avant*, an otiose exercise in the field of futurology.

5. ALTERNATIVES TO MACROECONOMIC POLICY CO-ORDINATION FOR FURTHER INTEGRATION, GROWTH AND A DEGREE OF POLICY AUTONOMY

The predicament of MERCOSUR countries is three-pronged. First of all, the intra-regional and extra-regional opening up to trade and capital flows has had serious consequences for a group of 'trade-sensitive' sectors of industry. Second, the pattern of exports to the rest of the world has not yet shifted towards industries capable of competing at a global level in dynamic sectors. And third, the lack of such industries has led to a chronic trade deficit which has been recently aggravated by the service burden on past financing of those very deficits, a situation that has put MERCOSUR countries in an extremely vulnerable position.

Therefore, both existing obstacles to intra-trade should be removed and a solid basis for all-round competitiveness should be built if MERCOSUR is to remain a force for growth.

First, 'the decks have to be cleared'; that is, any obstacles to intra-regional trade expansion have to be overcome. This is the decisive task for both the present and the foreseeable future. As has already been argued, however, success would require having to deal directly with the various partial conflicts at the sectoral level, and doing so in their own terms. The solution to these conflicts – those that have been causing ill feelings among members as well as producing counter-integration measures in the various countries – should be tackled via specific and not macroeconomic measures.

Second, vulnerability to world economic instability has to be overcome and sustainable long-run growth ensured at a regional level by developing more competitive industries in world terms. Otherwise, chronic trade and the ensuing current account deficits will result in a continuous dependence on fickle international private finance plus support from the international and regional financial institutions which deny a reasonable degree of policy autonomy to the countries of MERCOSUR. If anything is to be learned from the European Union experience, it is that Euroland countries entered into a currency union with a huge current account surplus of nearly US$100 billion per year. Notwithstanding such a fact, it is not clear whether a desired degree of policy autonomy has been fully achieved.

Third, and in the meantime, macroeconomic policies more aware of the 'trade-offs' between 'stability' and growth should be encouraged.

The first kind of highly prosaic issues are related to some 'trade-sensitive' sectors – quantitatively a small number – which have either potentially or actually been severely hit by trade liberalization within MERCOSUR.[18] Such issues have been putting economic policy makers with strong beliefs in favour of free trade in a quandary: defending liberalization up to the hilt, but ending up – in many cases – relapsing into the worst kind of protectionism, much of which is contrary to internationally accepted rules. Rather than such last-minute *ad hoc* protectionist measures, for this handful of 'sensitive' sectors explicit and transparent adjustment programmes have to be negotiated region-ally.

On the other hand, the only road towards gaining more autonomy and being able to enforce growth policies is the development of competitiveness, one which could lead to a less vulnerable position and to being integrated in the global economy, not only as a receiver of financial flows, but as a dynamic exporter as well. Thus, if the various national industrial strengths were put together in a bundle of activities that could be promoted at a regional level, this could help to overcome competitiveness problems in connection with the rest of the world.

In fact, both those conflicts regarding intra-regional integration and the lack of progress in achieving international competitiveness are, to some extent, the result of having applied only two of the instruments envisaged by the Treaty of Asunción, that is, intra-trade liberalization and the institution of a common external tariff. And, as discussed in this chapter, they will not be sorted out by a third one, macroeconomic policy coordination.

It is to a fourth – and rather forgotten – instrument of the Treaty of Asunción that our attention has to be drawn, that is, to 'sectoral' policies.[19] These policies should help to achieve an agreed restructuring of activities at a regional level that would dampen any damage that intra free trade might be generating. But more fundamentally, they would be the means of devising a policy of promoting – at that same level – some industries that offer the promise of achieving world-class competitiveness.

In both cases, rather than macroeconomic policy coordination, what is urgently needed in MERCOSUR is microeconomic policy coordination, the forgotten instrument envisaged by the Treaty of Asunción under the guise of 'sectoral policies'.

NOTES

1. This chapter is a transcript of a presentation made at St Antony's College, Oxford in June 2001 and thus does not deal with the effects on MERCOSUR of the Argentine crisis of late 2001 and the subsequent devaluation.
2. Intra-MERCOSUR exports over the period 1990–99 were growing at a rate of 15 per cent per year, much faster than the GDP of the region (3 per cent per year according to IADB Statistical and Quantitative Analysis Unit). In those same years, while world imports were growing at 6 per cent per year, MERCOSUR imports from the rest of the world were increasing at 12 per cent per year. See WTO, 'International Trade Statistics 2000', Tables I.3 and I.9.
3. Over the period 1990–99, for MERCOSUR and Latin American countries and the Caribbean, exports were increasing, respectively, at 5 and 8 per cent per year while imports

were growing, respectively, at 12 and 11 per cent per year. See WTO, 'International Trade Statistics 2000', Tables I.3 and I.9.

4. In the year 1998, at the peak of economic growth, trade balances (goods and services) were negative – 2.6 per cent of GDP on average – for each and every country in Latin America (19 countries) and current account deficits were running at an average rate of 4.5 per cent of GDP (CEPAL, 2001, ch. III, Table III.6).

5. External debt of Latin America and the Caribbean went up from $476 billion in 1990 to $793 billion at the end of 1999 (those figures represented, respectively, 40 and 46 per cent of aggregate GDP). In this last year total debt service was more than 8 per cent of GDP and almost 35 per cent of exports of goods and services. See The World Bank, 'Global Development Finance', CD-ROM 2000, summary tables.

6. While, in 1998, primary exports were less than a third of intra-MERCOSUR trade, they accounted for more than 55 per cent of exports to the rest of the world. Source: Author's own calculations on the basis of data provided from BADECEL, ECLA's Latin American trade database.

7. Of course, exports of wheat and oil from Argentina to Brazil are a significant element in trade between the two countries. There is, therefore, a widely disseminated view that Argentina is playing a 'colonial' role *vis-à-vis* Brazil, by exporting primary products and importing manufactured goods. But relative to the overall Argentine export composition, exports to Brazil show a much higher participation of manufactured products. Comparisons of 'revealed comparative advantage' of Argentina in different markets results in the same conclusion; that is, Argentina's exports to Brazil are much less 'colonial' than those to the rest of the world. See, for instance, O'Connell (2001).

8. Some agreements have developed in relation to purchases by Brazil of Argentine wheat and oil. Argentina grants some assurances of access to supplies in times of crisis and, on the other hand, Brazil provides a huge, neighbouring market for Argentine exports of those products. No special prices, however, are envisaged.

9. Compare, for instance, this situation with that of the European Union where Eire – the 'Celtic tiger' – was the recipient of aid from the EU of up to 6 per cent – gross – and 5 per cent – net – of its GDP.

10. The overvalued Argentine peso, however, used to attract a sizeable migration – not always legal in terms of immigration rules – from neighbouring countries including Paraguay, which is a member of MERCOSUR.

11. See S. Galiani and S. Nickell, 'Unemployment in Argentina in the 1990's'; mimeo, ITDT, as quoted by Levi Yeyati and Sturzenegger (1999).

12. See Heymann and Navajas (1998); and also Fundación Mediterránea (2000). In this last case the elasticity of Argentine exports to Brazil to Brazilian GDP is estimated to be 4.0 in the short run and 6.0 in the long run, while the absolute value of the elasticity towards the bilateral exchange rate was only 0.72.

13. In 1999, relative to the previous year, MERCOSUR imports from the rest of the world declined 14 per cent while those from the member countries fell 23 per cent. See O'Connell (2001).

14. See ibid.

15. Ibid., Tables 16–20.

16. See Rep. Argentina, Min. Economía, 'Indicadores Económicos; Apéndice 5, Sector Externo', May 2002.

17. For a similarly sceptical conclusion about the need for macroeconomic policy coordination in the case of Latin America, and most specifically of the MERCOSUR countries, see Loayza, Lopez and Ubide (1999).

18. In fact, in most cases, by trade liberalization *per se* but, again, it proved to be useful to blame, rather than international trade arrangements at large, the convenient scapegoat, that is, the neighbouring country, in all cases one which is smaller and thus a weaker power in world politics, consequently a less dangerous adversary than the major industrialized nations.

19. The Treaty of Asunción establishing MERCOSUR specifies four instruments for integration: (i) liberalization of intra-trade; (ii) macroeconomic policy coordination; (iii) setting up a

common external tariff and (iv) sectoral agreements. See Art. 5 of 'Tratado para la constitución de un mercado común entre la República Argentina, la República Federativa de Brasil, la República del Paraguay y la República Oriental del Uruguay'.

REFERENCES

CEPAL (2001), *Panorama de la Inserción Internacional de America Latina y el Caribe, 1999–2000*, Santiago de Chile: CEPAL, March.

Fundación Mediterránea (2000), 'Quo vadis, Real?' Buenos Aires: Fundación Mediterránea–IERAL, May.

Heymann D. and F. Navajas (1998), 'Coordinación de políticas macroeconómicas en MERCOSUR: algunas reflexiones', en Oficina de CEPAL en Buenos Aires, *Ensayos sobre la inserción internacional de la Argentina*, documento de Trabajo 81.

Levi Yeyati, E. and F. Sturzenegger (1999), 'The Euro and Latin America; III: Is EMU a Blueprint for MERCOSUR?', mimeo, April.

Loayza, N., H. Lopez and A. Ubide (1999), 'Sectorial Macroeconomic Interdependencies: Evidence for Latin America, East Asia and Europe', IMF Working Paper 99/11, January.

O'Connell, A. (2001), 'Los desafíos del MERCOSUR ante la devaluación de la moneda brasileña', serie *Estudios Estadísticos y Prospectivos*, no. 10, Santiago de Chile: CEPAL, February.

5. Monetary and exchange rate arrangements: a puzzle to be solved among major MERCOSUR countries

Maria L. Falcão Silva, Joaquim Pinto de Andrade and Hans-Michael Trautwein

1. INTRODUCTION

In recent years, the international economy has shifted from a bipolar world, dominated by the USA and the former Soviet Union, to a multipolar structure with three great economic powers – the European Union, Japan and the USA – and numerous other countries converging to regional economic blocs. In this new environment, Latin American countries are trying to strengthen relations among themselves. The most visible outcome of such efforts is MERCOSUR, the Common Market of the South created by an agreement between Argentina, Brazil, Uruguay and Paraguay, signed in 1991.

Processes of economic and monetary integration are never without problems. However, the problems are strongly magnified when member countries pursue different disinflationary stabilization programmes against a background of trade liberalization and financial market globalization, as has been the case in South America since the 1980s. The economic integration process in MERCOSUR is peculiar because its member countries have accepted a diversity of exchange rate arrangements, through which their currencies are linked to an outside currency in different ways. In particular, Argentina had its currency strictly fixed at a one-to-one parity with the US dollar between 1991 and early 2002, whereas Brazil ran more flexible exchange rate policies with several regime shifts in the same period. Given that Argentina and Brazil are by far the biggest member countries of MERCOSUR (and that the two, moreover, differ significantly in the size of their internal markets), trade integration and other aspects are likely to be obstructed by perverse effects of macroeconomic stabilization programmes under divergent monetary regimes.

This chapter explores the transmission of shocks in various constellations of exchange rate regimes that are described as alternative scenarios. Our main point is to show how the differences in monetary policies have contributed to the asynchronization and asymmetries in the cyclical fluctuations of economic activity in Argentina and Brazil. As Frankel and Rose (1997) have pointed out, positive correlations of subregional business cycles may be an outcome of monetary integration – and not necessarily an indispensable initial condition, as postulated by the optimal currency area (OCA) literature in the tradition of Mundell (1961). In other words, monetary integration may tend to make shocks more symmetric. Conversely, incompatible monetary policies may contribute to economic disintegration through the asynchronization of business cycles in the region. Along these lines, we show that symmetric shocks lead to uneven cycles due to asymmetries in the adjustment mechanisms of Argentina and Brazil. This leads to the conclusion that monetary policy is not neutral in the long run, since its repercussions affect the trade pattern and other real target variables of economic integration in MERCOSUR.

Following this introduction, the chapter is organized in four further sections. In the next two sections, we present empirical evidence of the relevant differences in the monetary and exchange rate policies of Argentina and Brazil. With hindsight, pointing out the inconsistency of monetary policies in the two countries may seem trivial, given the intra-MERCOSUR tensions in the period between spring 1999, when Brazil went on a floating exchange rate, and winter 2001/2, when Argentina had to abandon its quasi-currency-board arrangements. However, we show that the critical differences between the monetary regimes existed even at a time when both countries had the exchange rates of their currencies pegged to the dollar. After presenting the evidence, we examine different scenarios of policy interaction by making use of a general framework *à la* Mundell/Fleming. In the last section we summarize our main conclusions.

2. ARGENTINA'S RECENT EXPERIENCE WITH A QUASI-CURRENCY-BOARD ARRANGEMENT[1]

On 1 April 1991, Argentina's Congress approved a convertibility law (Law no. 23.929), institutionalizing a quasi-currency-board rule for monetary base creation. This law embodied the basic aspects of a currency board:

- it forced the central bank to confine its issue of the new domestic currency, the peso, almost exclusively to its holdings of foreign reserves in terms of US dollars;
- the official exchange rate established between the peso and the US dollar, the anchor currency, was fixed at one-to-one parity;
- the Central Bank of Argentina committed itself to guaranteeing the convertibility of 'peso notes and coins' into the anchor currency at the official rate.

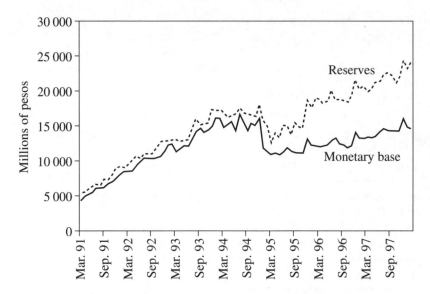

Source: Banco Central de la Republica Argentina, *Bulletins*, various issues.

Figure 5.1 Argentina: monetary base and foreign reserves, March 1991–February 1998 (in millions of pesos)

Figure 5.1 indicates the strict adherence of Argentina's monetary policy to these rules in the 'fat seven years', when the currency board experiment was widely considered a great success, because inflation was killed and the economy grew at an annual average of 6.07 per cent (Figure 5.7).

We have investigated the long-run properties of the relevant time series, foreign reserves and monetary base by making use of cointegration analysis. For estimation purposes, the variables are measured by their end-of-period balances and are taken on a monthly basis from reports of the Argentinean Central Bank. Monetary base (m) and foreign reserves (r) are considered in logarithmic form. Estimation is carried out for the period 1991:M3 to 1998:M2. From Table 5.1, all variables apparently yield an $I(1)$ process under both the ADF and the Phillips–Perron tests.

Estimation of an autoregressive distributed lag (ADL) yielded the following solved static long-run equation (figures in parentheses are standard errors):

$$m_t = 0.9628r_t - 0.74878 \ seasonal \qquad (5.1)$$
$$(0.0855335) \ (9.258)$$

Table 5.1   Unit root tests, Argentina

	M	R
I(0)		
DF	−0.056	0.524
ADF	0.051	0.559
I(1)		
DF	−3.703	−6.393
ADF	−3.434	−3.559

Note: The critical values for 5% and 1% levels of significance are −1.951 and −2.634, respectively.

Autoregressive distributed lags have error correction representations and our next step is to investigate the dynamic properties of our initial model using information from the preceding cointegration analysis. The Engle–Granger (1987) theorem establishes that if a group of variables forms a valid cointegration vector, it is possible to obtain a valid error correction representation which is not liable to the problem of spurious regression. Following the general-to-specific modelling strategy, our estimates of a parsimonious version of the ECM (error correction model) have yielded the following equation:

$$
\begin{aligned}
\Delta m_t = 0.111 &+ 0.4295\ \Delta r_t - 0.3065\ \Delta m_{t-2} - 0.0841\ sD_{95:1} \\
{\scriptstyle (0.022)}\ &\ {\scriptstyle (0.0916)}\qquad {\scriptstyle (0.0837)}\qquad\quad {\scriptstyle (0.0195)} \\
&- 0.1965 iD_{95:1} - 0.2789 ECM_{t-1} + S_{t-1} \\
&\ \ {\scriptstyle (0.0465)}\qquad {\scriptstyle (0.0669)}
\end{aligned}
\tag{5.2}
$$

AR 1 − 5F(5, 59) = 1.7961 [0.1276]	ARCH 5F(5, 54) = 0.592611 [0.7056]
Normality χ^2 (2) = 0.802838 [0.6694]	χ_i^2 F(19, 44) = 1.1371 [0.3511]
RESET F(1, 63) = 1.5989 [0.2107]	R^2 = 0.750 RSS = 0.0869
F(16, 64) = 12.021 DW = 2.40	

where S_t are 11 monthly seasonal dummies and ECM is the error correction term, which is obtained from the ADL solution above. In the short run, changes in monetary base balances respond to past months' excess demand (supply) increasing (decreasing) by 28 per cent, implying that short-run deviations from long-run equilibria were completely recovered after about three months. Note the importance of the step and impulse dummies for January 1995. It confirms the impression (from Figure 5.1) that monetary policy became even tighter after the contagious effects of the Mexican currency crisis at the end of 1994. The coefficient for the error correction term indicates remarkable stability.

The equation also presents numerous desirable statistical properties with favourable diagnostic tests: standard errors are in parentheses; AR $F(q, T - K - q)$ is the LM statistic for qth-order autocorrelation; ARCH $F(q, T - K - 2q)$ is the LM statistic qth-order ARCH; RESET is Ramsey's statistic for misspecification; and NORM χ^2 (2) is Jarque and Bera's statistic.

It should be noted that the long-run relationship is preserved, regardless of the changes in the short-run behaviour of the monetary basis *vis-à-vis* the foreign reserves (which are captured by the dummies added to the error correction model). The results of our cointegration analysis strongly support the notion that Argentina closely followed the quasi-currency-board rules during the period examined.

3. BRAZIL'S STERILIZATION POLICY[2]

The Real Plan, officially introduced on 1 July 1994, has been considered by several analysts as the most successful stabilization plan in Brazil's history. The main goal of the plan was the achievement of price stability and one of its principal elements was the nominal exchange rate anchor for the newly created currency unit, the real. Like the Argentinean peso, the parity between the real and the US dollar was established at a one-to-one exchange rate. According to Law no. 9.069 (approved on 29 June 1994), monetary policy was designed to keep the money supply in line with the US dollar reserves. However, the relationship between changes in monetary base and movements in foreign reserves was not explicitly stated, and the exchange rate was permitted to move within a target band. The Real Plan thus allowed some degree of discretion.

Figure 5.2 shows clearly that the monetary base and domestic credit in Brazil rarely followed the foreign reserves pattern during the 1980s and 1990s. In comparison with Argentina, it is worth noting that the monetary base was kept almost constant during the critical period after the Mexican crisis (January–April 1995). Analysing the conditioning components of the monetary base – domestic credit (*cre*) and foreign reserves (*r*) – one cannot avoid the conclusion that open-market operations were carried out to offset the negative pressure of the decline in the foreign reserves. When, on the other hand, the foreign reserves position was improved in the second half of 1996, the monetary base was kept more or less constant. The insulation of the monetary base from the movements of the foreign reserves, illustrated by Figure 5.2, is remarkable. The absence of co-movements between the two series confirms the discretionary character of the Brazilian monetary policy.[3] Even though

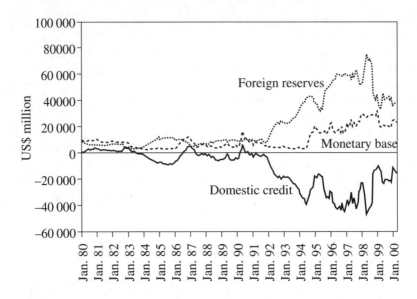

Source: Authors' estimation based on data published in *Boletim do Banco Central do Brasil*,
various issues.

*Figure 5.2   Brazil: monetary base, domestic credit and foreign reserves,
1980–2000 (in millions of US dollars)*

such discretion is frequently considered to be detrimental to the credibility of
the central bank, it was apparently consistent with a strategy to finance imports
by attracting high inflows of foreign capital.

Here, as in the Argentine experiment, it is worth investigating the long-run
properties of these time series, proceeding to a cointegration analysis of
domestic credit and foreign reserves. For estimation purposes, the variables
are measured in current US dollars by their end-of-period balances and are
taken on a monthly basis from reports of the Brazilian Central Bank.

From Table 5.2, all variables apparently yield an $I(1)$ process under both the
ADF and the Phillips–Perron tests.

Estimation is carried out for three different periods: (a) the whole sample,
1980:M1 to 2000:M3; (b) a first subsample, 1980:M1 to 1990:M2; and (c) a third
subsample, 1990:M3 to 2000:M3. The definitions of the two subsamples is based
on the analysis of the residuals and the Chow test of an ADL that reveals that
there is a significant structural change in 1990, as can be seen in Figure 5.3 below.
The assumption is that there was a significant change in monetary policy that
started with the emergency measures against hyperinflation and the Collor II Plan
in 1990, and that was reinforced by the implementation of the Real Plan in 1994.

Table 5.2   Unit root tests, Brazil

	cre	r	residuals
I(0)			
PP	−0.8637	0.4667	−9.6239
ADF	−1.0626	0.2495	−5.7732
I(1)			
PP	−8.8155	−6.7343	
ADF	−4.1249	−4.1610	

Note: The critical values for 5% and 1% levels of significance are −2.88 and −3.49, respectively.

The model for the whole sample yielded the following results:

$$cre = +17.33 - 0.7202r + 0.3237\ sD_{98:1} + seasonals$$
$$\underset{(SE)}{}\ \underset{(1.186)}{}\ \underset{(0.1252)}{}\ \underset{(0.3528)}{} \tag{5.3}$$

Nevertheless, observation of Figure 5.3 suggests a strong change of regime around 1990. For that reason we estimated the same model for two different samples as related above.

A long-run *equilibrium* relationship between credit and foreign reserves defines the monetary policy of the first period: 1980:M1 to 1990:M2 according to the following results:

$$cre = 11.95 - 0.1158r - 0.002862\ trend + 0.172\ sD_{86:2} + seasonals$$
$$\underset{(0.1183)}{}\ \underset{(0.01338)}{}\ \underset{(0.0002271)}{}\ \underset{(0.01455)}{} \tag{5.4}$$

The short-run relationship with the error correction mechanism is estimated and confirms the existence of the long-run equilibrium. The error correction mechanism shows that the adjustment towards a long-run equilibrium takes about one year.

$$\Delta cre = 0.006 + 0.358\ \Delta cre_{-1} - 0.182\ \Delta r + 0.049\ (r_{-1} + 0.023\ \Delta r_{-2}$$
$$\underset{(0.004)}{}\ \underset{(0.08)}{}\ \underset{(0.015)}{}\ \underset{(0.02)}{}\ \underset{(0.015)}{}$$
$$+ seasonals + 0.002\ sD_{86:2} - 0.212ECM$$
$$\underset{(0.002)}{}\ \underset{(0.04)}{} \tag{5.5}$$

AR 1 − 7F(7, 94) = 0.70593 [0.6670]	ARCH 7F(7, 87) = 1.0442 [0.4066]
Normality χ^2 (2) = 0.03133 [0.9845]	$\chi_i^2 F$(22, 78) = 1.6797 [0.0501]
RESET F(1, 100) = 0.73061 [0.3947]	

The statistical properties of the model present the desired properties.

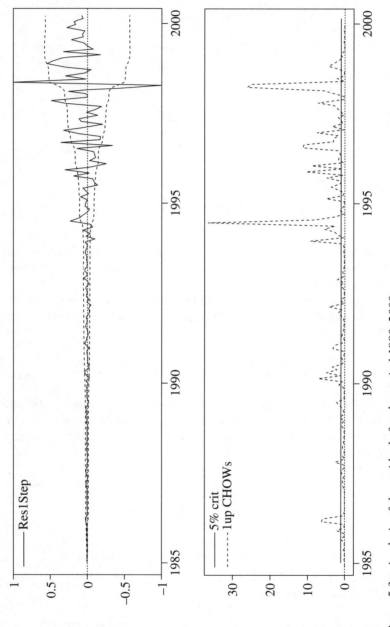

Figure 5.3   Analysis of the residuals for the period 1980–2000

The short-run relationship can be understood as a policy reaction function pursued by the monetary authorities. The short-run coefficient of change of credits on change of reserves indicates that about 17 per cent of the inflow of reserves is sterilized. The existence of the long-run relationship in equation (5.4) may express the effectiveness of the sterilization policy.[4]

The period that started with the Collor disinflation measures in March 1990 indicates a change in the long-run relationship between domestic credit and foreign reserves. The long-run coefficient of credit on reserves that was around (–0.12) jumps to (–0.9), as can be read from equation (5.6).

$$cre = 18.98 - 0.8636r + 0.2293iD_{98:1} + seasonals \tag{5.6}$$
$$ (1.553) \quad (0.1497) \quad (0.236)$$

The error correction mechanism of the short-run relationship confirms the existence of the long-run relationship of equation (5.6) and denotes a substantial change in the credit policy reaction function. The short-run sterilization coefficient reaches (–1.6).

$$\Delta cre = 0.126 + 0.191\,\Delta cre_{-3} - 1.589\,\Delta r - 1.319iD_{98:4} - 0.518\,iD_{98:3}$$
$$ (0.068) \quad (0.067) \quad\quad (0.244) \quad\quad (0.193) \quad\quad (0.194)$$
$$+ 0.385iD_{96:9} - 0.758iD_{96:10} - 0.295ECM + seasonals \tag{5.7}$$
$$ (0.195) \quad\quad (0.192) \quad\quad (0.052)$$

AR 1 – 7$F(7, 73)$ = 2.7446 [0.0138]	ARCH 7$F(7, 66)$ = 1.5478 [0.1668]
Normality $\chi^2 (2)$ = 1.5258 [0.4663]	$\chi_i^2\,F(21, 58)$ = 1.0529 [0.4211]
RESET $F(1, 79)$ = 8.0106 [0.0059]	

In the short run the monetary authorities tend to overshoot: on top of the 100 per cent of the inflow of foreign reserves that is sterilized an additional amount of domestic assets is sold, corresponding to about 60 per cent of the original inflow. Nevertheless, the adjustment to the long-run sterilization coefficient however is very rapid and takes only four months.

These results confirm that Brazilian monetary policy has tended to insulate the development of domestic monetary aggregates from changes in foreign reserves. They also show that there was a significant structural change in the sterilization policy pursued by the monetary authorities. The existence of a negative long-run relationship between credit and foreign reserves suggests that there was some scope for independent monetary policy even with a moving target band.[5]

4.   EXCHANGE RATE REGIMES WITHIN MERCOSUR

This section introduces a general framework *à la* Mundell/Fleming which serves to examine the transmission of various types of shocks under alternative scenarios of exchange rate arrangements within and among countries. Despite its well-known limitations, this kind of framework is useful for shedding some light on the inconsistency problems that may arise when countries engaged in trade integration pursue different monetary policies in various constellations of exchange rate regimes.

Let us consider three scenarios (or 'thought experiments') with three hypothetical economies (we can imagine *A* to be Argentina, *B* Brazil, and *C* the USA or the rest of the world):[6]

scenario 1: fixed exchange rates *A/B*, *A/C* and *B/C*,
scenario 2: fixed exchange rate *A/C*, floating exchange rates *B/A* and *B/C*,
scenario 3: a target zone for exchange rates *A/B*, fixed exchange rates *A/C*.

Before discussing the scenarios, we follow Krugman and Obstfeld (1994) and Argy (1994) in sketching a simple model that we use to develop our analysis of the transmission of shocks. Different cases will be explored related to alternative exchange rate arrangements among the countries involved. The model is based on the following equations:

$$Y_A = D_A(Y_B, r_A, Y_C^*, e, f_A) \tag{5.8}$$

$$Y_B = D_B(Y_A, r_B, Y_C^*, e, f_B) \tag{5.9}$$

$$M_A = L(Y_A, r_A) \tag{5.10}$$

$$M_B = L(Y_B, r_B) \tag{5.11}$$

$$M_B = \bar{M}_B \tag{5.12}$$

$$r_A = r_B \tag{5.13}$$

$$0 = BP_B(Y_B, Y_A, Y_C^*, e, r_B - r_c) \tag{5.14}$$

$$e = \bar{e} \tag{5.15}$$

Y denotes output and *M* is real money supply, *r* denotes interest rate, *f* is the fiscal variable and *e* is the real exchange rate. Equations (5.8) and (5.9) represent equilibrium in the goods markets (*IS*). Equations (5.10), (5.11) and (5.12) represent equilibrium in the money markets (*LM*). Equation (5.12) indicates that country *B* controls the money supply either by sterilization, when the exchange rate is fixed, or by permitting it to float. Equation (5.13) represents the equilibrium condition for the foreign exchange market. Equations (5.14) and (5.15) stand, respectively, for the balance-of-payments equilibrium condition under a floating exchange rate, conventionally taken to be necessary for determining the latter's value, and for the target level of the exchange rate under a fixed exchange rate system. The assumption is that perfect capital mobility prevails between countries *A* and *B*, and that domestic prices in both countries are fixed or sticky in the short run.

Scenario 1   Assume that a credible fixed exchange rate arrangement prevails among the three countries. Consider the integration area (*A* + *B*). The effects of monetary and fiscal policies will be more important from *B* to *A* than from *A* to *B*, if *A* depends more on *B* than *B* does on *A*. This is due to the lack of symmetry (in size and/or structure) between the two economies.

Assume now that *B* makes use of sterilization practices (open-market operations by which *B* tries to offset the impacts of foreign reserves changes on the monetary base), while economy *A* does not sterilize. Take *C*'s position as given (*ceteris paribus*). Consider that perfect capital mobility prevails between *A* and *B*, but that it is less than perfect in relation to *C*. These assumptions enable us to set the focus on the relationship between *A* and *B*.

If the scenario is the one described above, economy *B* starts to play the dominant role in terms of controlling monetary policy. Changes in monetary policy in *A* affect *B*'s level of reserves, but not its money supply. The question is: will country *A* accept a monetary policy dictated by country *B*? (Keep in mind that, in this example, *B* stands for Brazil and *A* for Argentina!) The loss of autonomy on the part of *A* seems to be the main problem of this relationship.

Domestic policies originating in Brazil   Monetary shocks originating in Brazil will increase the money supply in both countries, as illustrated by the rightward shifts of the *LM* curves in Figure 5.4. The result is a decline of the region's interest rate followed by an expansion of output in both economies (points 2 and 2). On the other hand, monetary shocks originating in Argentina will be dampened in Brazil and therefore in Argentina as well. The sterilization policy implemented by Brazil creates an important asymmetry in this relationship.

Within the same thought experiment it is interesting to recall the effects of sterilization upon the transmission of fiscal shocks. Fiscal shocks originating in Brazil will be expansionary in Brazil and contractionary in Argentina. Figure 5.4 illustrates this case. Points 0 and 0 mark the initial equilibria in the output and foreign exchange markets of both economies. The fiscal shock

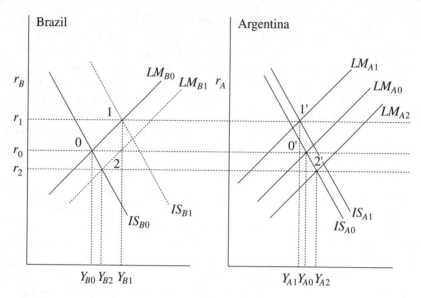

Figure 5.4   Monetary and fiscal expansion in Brazil

originating in *B* shifts the *IS* curve to the right and determines a new equilibrium (point 1) in which *B*'s output (Y_{B1}) and interest rate (r_1) are higher. Due to rising demand for *A*'s exports, IS_A will also shift to the right. However, interest arbitrage in the foreign exchange market will lead to an outflow of reserves from *A* to *B* until equation (5.13) holds. Open market sterilization policy ensures that the Brazilian money supply does not change. As a result the interest rate in the region will remain at r_1, leading to a fall in Argentina's output (Y_{A1}) as *LM* contracts to the new equilibrium (at point 1).

Domestic policies originating in Argentina   By adopting a fixed exchange rate regime without sterilization, *A* loses its capacity to conduct an independent monetary policy. In this case, fiscal policy becomes more powerful. Suppose that Argentina undertakes a fiscal expansion, as illustrated by Figure 5.5. The outcome in *A* will be an expansion in the aggregate demand (IS_A shifts to the right). As a result the output in *A* will increase ($Y_{A1} - Y_{A0}$), followed by a rise in the interest rate to r_1. This will have positive effects on Brazil through trade (IS_B shifts to the right) and negative effects through capital outflows to *A* (LM_B shifts to the left). The equilibria at points 1 and 1 are not stable, however, because the monetary leakage in *B* is neutralized by the central bank. Together with capital flows from *C* to *A*, those leakages will further enhance the positive effect of *A*'s fiscal expansion. In the final equilibrium (points 2 and 2), the interest rate will return to its initial level r_0. In other words, fiscal shocks coming from Argentina do not lead to a crowding out of private investment.

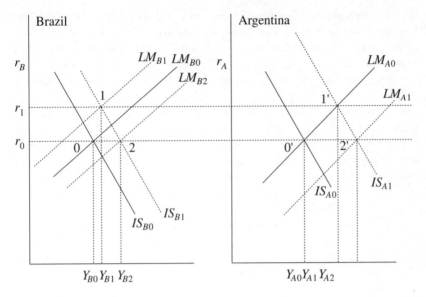

Figure 5.5   Fiscal expansion in Argentina

Due to the fixed exchange rate arrangement, there is no exchange rate crowding out, and the interest-rate crowding out disappears due to the sterilization policy in *B*. In this way, the fiscal shock coming from *A* is amplified.

The main result is the existence of a trade-off in Argentinean stabilization policy: the loss of the monetary policy instrument is compensated by the gain in the effectiveness of fiscal policy, since there is no interest rate crowding out.

Shocks originating in the rest of the world   This analysis has to contemplate the response of the region to external shocks. Fixed exchange rate systems translate any change in foreign demand into internal shocks. For instance, a reduction of exports will have effects very similar to those of a reduction in government expenditures. In the same way, any change in net capital flows between *C* and the *A* + *B* region corresponds to changes in the money supply of the countries in the region. In the case of Argentina and Brazil, however, it may be argued that, in the period between 1994 and 1999, the different monetary policies should have had a symmetric positive effect on the stability of aggregate demand in the region. Consider, for example, the reserve shock in the wake of the Mexican crisis 1994–95: both Argentina and Brazil lost nearly one-third of their foreign reserves within a few weeks (see Figures 5.1 and 5.2). It is conceivable that Argentina would have lost far more reserves and would not have regained them so quickly, had the country not enjoyed the credibility bonus of the currency board system. Brazil, on the other hand, could not exploit such a bonus, as the Mexican crisis came only a few months after the Real Plan – time was too short to establish credibility. But the Brazilian Central Bank mitigated the reserve shock by keeping the money supply stable. In this process, the Brazilian monetary policy may even have helped to dampen the effects of the reserve shock on Argentina, in so far as arbitrage-related capital flows from Brazil to Argentina compensated for some of the capital flight from Argentina to the rest of the world.

Our analysis in the preceding sections has shown that both Argentina and Brazil pursued tight money policies when large capital inflows to the region led to strong increases in reserve holdings in 1995–96. This restrictive stance may be explained as attempts to gain and preserve credibility, but it is hard to avoid the conclusion that it has contributed to the recession that befell the region in the late 1990s. A new and even stronger type of monetary asymmetry developed, when Brazil could no longer neutralize the capital outflows that it suffered after the Asian and Russian crises in 1997–98, in a period of intra-Brazilian haggling over the stance of fiscal policy. Brazil switched to a floating exchange rate, whereas Argentina preferred to stick to the currency board. This brings us to the next scenario.

Scenario 2   Suppose the region were to shift from a fixed exchange rate arrangement to a floating exchange rate regime. Assume, however, that a fixed exchange rate arrangement prevails between *A* and *C* (as it did occur in reality between the Argentine peso and the US dollar from 1991 to January 2002), while *B*'s currency floats in relation to *C*'s and *A*'s currencies (as in Brazil after January 1999).

Shock amplification mechanism   An interesting aspect to be pointed out has to do with the vulnerability to external shocks. As the analysis of Scenario 1 suggests, *A* becomes more vulnerable to external shocks than *B*, given its commitment to a fixed exchange rate *a*. In the case of *B*, floating exchange rates insulate, partly, the effects of foreign shocks in the same way that sterilization policy does. On the other hand, demand shocks that affect *B* will be transmitted to *A* through movements of the exchange rate. Floating thus modifies the interaction between Brazil's independent monetary policy and the currency board system in Argentina to the extent that the basic asymmetry is extended to the effects of external shocks. Figure 5.6 illustrates these effects, showing the impact of a shock that affects both Argentina and Brazil. It shows that Argentina ends up being hit twice: first directly and then indirectly through the devaluation of Brazil's currency.

Shocks that hit Argentina   Assume a situation in which an external shock is represented by an increase in commodity prices in the world market (ε). As its terms of trade are worsened, Argentina will face external disequilibria with a current account deficit and a decline in foreign reserves. The adjustment mechanism designed by a currency board arrangement will lead to a reduction

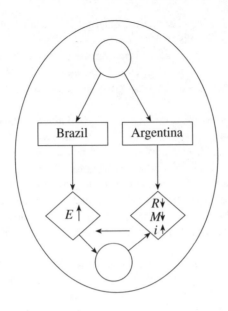

Notes:
Suppose that: ε and v are external shocks
E: nominal exchange rate
R: international reserves
M: monetary base
i: interest rate
The arrows represent causation. The arrows inside the figures represent change of the level of the variables.

Figure 5.6   The double impact of external shocks on Argentina

of the monetary base, with a consequent rise of the interest rate. Two main effects should follow from that: one is the stagnation of GDP in *A*; the other, less important, is the inflow of capital from *C* (the rest of the world) and, particularly, from *B*. The first one corresponds to the direct translation of a foreign shock into an internal shock and is likely to have serious consequences in terms of unemployment. The second is of small order but may add to the direct effect on *A*, because the outflow of capital from *B* could lead to a devaluation of *B*'s currency which, in turn, could increase the current account deficit of *A*.

Shocks that hit Argentina and Brazil   Consider that the same shock also hits Brazil, leading to an external imbalance. None the less, in this case, the adjustment mechanism of the Brazilian exchange rate regime will smooth the external shock through devaluation. This procedure translates itself into an external shock to Argentina's economy (v), leading to the same consequences as described above. In other words, external shocks that hit *B* will generate secondary external shocks to *A*.

The transmission of the shocks among the countries becomes asymmetrical. The shocks are smoothed in Brazil and amplified in Argentina. As indicated before, this mechanism may generate a vicious circle that precludes convergence.

Credibility shocks affecting Argentina   It is interesting to understand the effects of credibility shocks in Argentina. When investors lose confidence in *A*'s sustainability of the currency board regime the model suggests that capital will flow out of *A*. This may have contagious effects on *B* in the sense that investors' imperfect information will lead them to reduce their engagements in *B* too. This credibility shock may set a cumulative process in motion that goes from *A* to *B* and back to *A*. Capital outflows from Argentina will be followed by capital outflows from Brazil and, as a consequence, the Brazilian currency will be devaluated.

Differences in monetary and exchange rate policies   The differences in monetary and exchange rate policies correspond to different mechanisms of adjustment to negative external shocks. Currency board arrangements rely mainly on monetary adjustments that tend to produce output changes, at least in the short run. On the other hand, floating regimes adjust through the currency market, that is, through price adjustments. While price mechanisms may, to some extent, insulate the economies from external shocks, monetary mechanisms lead to considerable quantity adjustments. The interrelationship between price and quantity adjustments may create an unstable system.

Any non-coordinated change in *A* or *B* can thus affect the degree of their trade integration through the channel of monetary policy. Assume, for example, that a monetary contraction in *A* leads to a devaluation of *B*'s currency in relation to *A*'s. The effect will take the form of a trade shift. *A* will import more from and export less to *B*. But the level of trade may also be affected, if a contraction in *A*'s income leads to lower imports from *B*. This may induce further devaluations of *B*'s currency, if not a downward spiral of trade in the region.

Scenario 3   The last scenario to be explored represents an extension of the last possibility of scenario 2 and considers the implementation of a target zone exchange rate arrangement in *B* and also between *A* and *B*. Assume that the fixed exchange rate regime between *A* and C is maintained.

Target zones impose constraints on the fiscal and monetary policies of country *B* (especially if they are combined with a fixed exchange rate of *A* with some external currency). Consider the case in which *B* has a fiscal deficit that is permanently higher than that of *A* and/or *C*. In our simple Mundell/Fleming framework that would translate into a rate of interest that tends to be too high, and an exchange rate that is too low. *B* will be pushed to the lower limit of the exchange rate band and to the upper limit of the (implicit) interest rate band. Monetary policy is tight, in the sense that it is not used to finance the fiscal deficit, and capital inflows are mostly sterilized, but in the meantime *B* would accumulate a trade balance deficit in relation to both *A* and the rest of the world. If financial market investors begin to doubt the sustainability of the exchange rate, a speculative attack *à la* Krugman (1979) on the foreign reserves of *B* is likely to occur – with consequences that bring us back to the integration problems of scenario 2. Note that this kind of exercise is slightly different from the traditional one in which the speculative attack is due to the expansion of internal credit. Here fiscal imbalances point to an overvaluation of the domestic exchange rate, and to a trade balance disequilibrium. Its sustainability would depend on the confidence that financial markets have in the country's economic policies. It is well worth noting that scenario 3 bears some resemblance to the situation of Brazil before and during the currency crisis of 1999 that forced the country to switch to floating exchange rates.

5.   CONCLUSION

Our scenarios of alternative exchange rate arrangements for MERCOSUR countries suggest that the coexistence of Argentina's fixed exchange rate regime based on currency board rules and Brazil's more independent policies has created obstacles to economic integration in the MERCOSUR region. When both countries had fixed their exchange rates in terms of the US dollar, domestic policy shocks tended to produce asymmetric adjustments, because Brazil largely neutralized the impact of intra-regional capital flows, whereas Argentina did not. In this constellation, trade integration would be favoured only by monetary expansion in Brazil or by fiscal expansion in Argentina; the difference in the monetary policy regimes may nevertheless have helped to buffer external shocks, as in the case of the Mexican crisis. However, the underlying asymmetry was exacerbated when Brazil switched to floating in 1999. Now even external shocks had clearly adverse effects on trade integration and the synchronization of economic development in the region. They worked their way through the two economies in a fashion that caused Argentina to be hit twice – first by the original shock and thereafter by its repercussions through devaluations of the Brazilian currency. The asymmetries following from the different monetary and exchange rate arrangements have generated an increasing divergence in the patterns of output fluctuation that is illustrated by Figure 5.7.

The lack of macroeconomic policy coordination in MERCOSUR has led to

Sources: INDEC and IBGE.

Figure 5.7   GDP growth in Argentina and Brazil, 1991–2001

serious setbacks in the process of trade integration. The devaluation of the Brazilian real and the severe contraction of aggregate demand in Argentina have produced strong negative effects on the productive capacity of the Argentinean economy – an experience that hardly makes a good base for further economic integration. On the contrary, monetary disintegration has spurred conflicts over remaining trade barriers in the region that might otherwise have been eliminated long ago. Argentina has accused Brazil of pursuing a 'beggar thy neighbour' policy, but it has finally had to accept that its own policy of 'beggar the IMF by sticking to the currency board' was unsustainable. In January 2002, the peso was officially devaluated by 30 per cent and the convertibility law was suspended.

At the time of writing this chapter (January 2002), the situation was too unstable to allow any predictions about the future course of monetary policies in MERCOSUR. Macroeconomic policy coordination between the member countries is certainly a must in the longer run. An arrangement with target zones for exchange rates in MERCOSUR is probably one of the few remaining options. Yet this is not without problems either, as scenario 3 of our analysis indicates. How to switch from the vicious circle of monetary disintegration to a virtuous circle of macroeconomic convergence and trade integration that is both required for and sustained by target zone arrangements is a puzzle to be solved by the two major MERCOSUR countries.

NOTES

1. This subsection follows closely Silva (1999) and Andrade, Silva and Carneiro (2000).
2. For a detailed analysis see Andrade, Silva and Carneiro (2000).
3. It should be noted, however, that hyperinflation was eliminated in the second half of 1994. Not surprisingly, this period was marked by a strong process of monetization of portfolios, in which case the portfolio changes tend to bear very little direct relation to foreign reserves.
4. On sterilization policy and its effects on exchange rates and monetary aggregates see Edison (1993).
5. It has been suggested that the exchange rate regime adopted by Brazil in the first stages of the Real Plan was a crawling peg and not target bands as officially announced; see Pastore and Pinotti (1999).
6. These exercises are applications of Mundell–Fleming type models for two and three countries. See Argy (1994), pp. 150–93.

REFERENCES

Andrade, J.P., M.L. Falcão Silva and F.G. Carneiro (2000), 'Contrasting Monetary Policies within the MERCOSUR experiment', *Economia Aplicada*, **4** (2), 223–51.
Argy, Vitor (1994), *International Macroeconomics: Theory and Policy*, London and New York: Routledge.
Banco Central de La República Argentina, *Bulletins*, various issues.
Banco Central do Brasil, *Boletim do Banco Central do Brasil*, various issues.
Edison, H.J. (1993), 'The Effectiveness of Central-Bank Intervention: A Survey of the Literature After 1982', *Princeton Special Papers in International Economics*, **18**.
Frankel, J.A and A.K. Rose (1997), 'The Endogeneity of the Optimum Currency-Area Criteria', *Swedish Economic Policy Review*, **4**, 487–512.
Engle, R.F. and C.W.J. Granger (1987), 'Co-integration and error correction: representation, estimation and testing', *Econometrica*, **55**, 251–76.
International Monetary Fund, *International Financial Statistics*, various issues.
Krugman, P. (1979), 'A Model of Balance of Payments Crises', *Journal of Money, Credit, and Banking*, **11**, 311–25.
Krugman, Paul and Maurice Obstfeld (1994), *International Economics: Theory and Practice*, 3rd edn, New York: HarperCollins College Publishers.
Mundell, R.A. (1961), 'A Theory of Optimum Currency Areas', *The American Economic Review*, **51**, 657–65.
Pastore, A. and M.C. Pinotti (1999), 'Inflação e Estabilização: Algumas lições da Experiência Brasileira', *Revista Brasileira de Economia*, **53** (1), 3–40.
Silva, Maria Luiza Falcão (1999), *Modern Exchange-Rate Regimes, Stabilisation Programmes and Co-ordination of Macroeconomic Policies*, Aldershot, UK and Vermont, USA: Ashgate Publishing Company, pp. 186–98.

6. Some issues on the financial/monetary integration of MERCOSUR*

Adriana Moreira Amado and Luiz Afonso Simoens da Silva

INTRODUCTION

Financial globalization has been influential in terms of its impact on the monetary dynamics of national economies. Segmented markets in geo-political or in product terms come together to create bigger but fewer markets, where the influential areas are relatively well defined (Carvalho, 1997b). The impact on the dynamics of this process is not obvious. On the one hand, it could be thought of as creating new opportunities for finance, which would enhance economic growth at the international level (ibid.). On the other hand, it could lead to a distinct separation of the financial sphere from the real side of the economy, strengthening the former and weakening the latter. This would have negative effects on growth potential, especially if proper account is taken of speculative behaviour in the financial markets and the instability this may create (Plihon, 1995).

Globalization has been followed by a more radical process, that of opening up domestic economies via the formation of economic blocs. At the same time, the emergence of these blocs is one way for these countries to be involved more closely in the international scenario of globalization.[1] Among the various attempts at economic integration the European Union is the most advanced. It has reached the stage of actually implementing an Economic and Monetary Union (EMU).[2] The relevant notion, when dealing with economic issues, that concerns country members of the EMU is clearly more related to regional rather than to national issues, since there are no barriers to free movement of goods, factors and capital within the EMU area.

Analysing nations as different political blocs implies certain legal frictions that slow down the strength and intensity of the economic relations between countries. Among them there are barriers to capital, labour and goods. Thus, economic relations among regions are under fewer restrictions than among nations. This means that market mechanisms that lead to convergence or divergence act much more rapidly and intensively on a regional than on an international level (Amado, 1997).

In terms of monetary unions, the only bloc that has managed to reach the regional level is the European EMU. However, globalization has promoted a certain kind of financial integration through the internationalization of financial systems. When the recent process of denationalization of the Brazilian financial system is analysed, it can easily be seen that the strategy of foreign banks is not only is concerned with the Brazilian market, but is much more associated with developments on the MERCOSUR front (Amado, 1998). This 'spontaneous' process of financial integration is problematic in that it is undertaken in an uncontrolled way and without the requirements and preconditions that are assumed to prevail in economic blocs which deliberately proceed to monetary/financial integration. In the case of a 'spontaneous' process, market mechanisms that generate vicious circles and amplify and perpetuate regional inequality tend to be emphasized.

This chapter analyses the new financial dynamic known as MERCOSUR.[3] In this, policy makers are faced with the possibility of a new phase in the integration process where the financial integration will be, inevitably, one of the main issues.[4] In Brazil, the discussion on the possibility of a monetary integration within MERCOSUR has been based on the European EMU model, which originated in Mundell (1961) and assumes neutrality of money. The financial system is seen as a neutral element that merely intermediates between savers and investors.[5] Analysis which assumes non-neutrality of money has not yet been developed for MERCOSUR,[6] at least up to publication of this book – clearly there is plenty in this book that is based on non-neutrality of money.

The analysis undertaken in this chapter is based firmly on a Post-Keynesian perspective. It assumes that money has an important influence on the pattern of growth of the economy. This assumption, and the way in which financial integration is done, can change the relative patterns of growth of the national economies within the bloc.

1.   THEORETICAL FRAMEWORK

This section analyses money as an essential element in understanding the dynamics of accumulation of monetary production economies. In doing so, we will assume historical time, radical uncertainty and, consequently, money will be seen as a socially created element that allows agents to act in a world similar to the one depicted above. Liquidity preference will be, therefore, a rational result. Money will be analysed as an endogenous element, not only for its origin and role in social cohesion, but also because it is created within the system and its supply can be explained by the rational behaviour of the banking sector jointly with the monetary authority. As a consequence, banks have a fundamental role to play in this model, because in the last analysis they are the main institution responsible for liquidity creation. Since liquidity is one of the main constraints to growth, their behaviour explains growth patterns to a very large extent.

As the chapter is concerned with economic integration in blocs and financial liberalization inside those blocs, it will assume models that are close to the regional monetary/financial dynamic in a Post-Keynesian approach. These models were developed by Dow (1985, 1987) and Chick and Dow (1988, 1994) and more recently have been used by the authors to analyse the European Monetary Union case, in view of the similarities that monetary unions generate in relation to regional economies.

Assuming time in its historical perspective, that is, as a variable that is unidirectional and goes from the past to the future without any possibility of reversion, Chick and Dow (1988)[7] point to the irreversible character of the decision-making process, and its creative character in relation to the future. That is, the future cannot be perfectly predicted from the past. Uncertainty, which is a consequence of these two elements – irreversibility and creativity – in a monetary production economy, is a fundamental element in the decision-making process. Since liquidity preference represents a safe haven, in view of the fact that liquid assets allow perfect mobility and flexibility for adapting to new situations, it is the consequence of two elements: historical time and uncertainty.

In this way, the decision-making process should be based on elements that are not restricted to past events only. There should be room for surprise, which is fundamental to decision-making agents. Since they cannot foresee the future with certainty, they tend to use convention as a good guide to the decision-making process. Considering economies that have different levels of uncertainty and instability, agents tend to present different levels of liquidity preference in each economy and at each moment in time. This can be observed not only at a household level but also at the level of firms and banks.

If the interest rate is considered the price necessary to pay for agents to depart from liquidity and, at the same time, it is observed as the limit given to investment in relation to the marginal efficiency of capital, economies in which agents have a higher liquidity preference tend to have lower investment levels than those in which agents are faced with lower liquidity preference. Consequently, there will be more constrained patterns of growth. If we are dealing with closed economies, this tendency is weaker than with open economies. In open economies the higher liquidity preference of depressed and more unstable regions, that is the periphery, tend to be manifested in the demand for assets of the core regions since they are more liquid.

In the periphery, there are leakages of finance that are an inherent characteristic of these regions. Banks prefer to extend loans to core regions, especially if they have their head offices there, since the base for information in the periphery is more volatile than that in the core. This amplifies the shortage of liquidity in the depressed regions. Moreover, given the higher liquidity preference of these regions, this pressure is also observed on the demand side of the liquidity schedule. The joint analysis of these elements emphasizes the liquidity constraint on the potential of growth in the periphery.

Another element that emphasizes the scarcity of liquidity in peripheral economies is associated with the different money multipliers in regional terms. As the money supply can be considered endogenous at a regional level, since there are financial and monetary flows among regions, the regional money multiplier depends on the liquidity preference, in the same way that it depends, at a national level, on the leakages that originated in the balance of trade among regions and by the financial flows between regions. The analysis demonstrates that liquidity preference and leakages, real and financial, tend to be larger in the peripheral than in the core regions. The implication of this analysis is that there are lower money multipliers in the periphery than in the core. On the other hand, banks tend to be more restrictive in peripheral regions, in terms of their voluntary reserve ratios, since the higher uncertainty of these economies forces them to keep safer positions.

Peripheral regions tend to have lower money multipliers. This gives a comparative advantage to banks that operate in the core in comparison with those that operate in the periphery, which strengthens the tendency towards banking concentration. This intensifies the financial shortage in the periphery, because credit creation in this region by core banks has a more volatile base than the one in periphery banks. This reduces the availability of finance, amplifying the gap of development among the regions.

Banks with head offices in core regions, and those that operate in the periphery, tend to extend loans to the periphery through firms that also have head offices in the core and normally operate nation-wide. The structure of these firms means that they face higher linkages with the region where they have their head offices, which is the core region. This contributes to higher leakages in the income multiplier of the peripheral regions, as the input necessary for production and the capital goods necessary for investment represent demand, almost exclusively to the core region. This worsens the trade balance of these regions and generates an extra source of financial leakage from the periphery.

Summing up, financial systems in situations of deep structural diversity tend to reinforce the initial regional inequality in terms of development levels. Financial liberalization processes, led by the market rationale, do not take into account this fact and do not erect barriers to the free movement of capital. As a result they amplify inequality among countries of regional blocs. The case studied by Chick and Dow (1996), Europe, is much closer to their model, since it began from the notion of core and periphery, than to the MERCOSUR case. Regional imbalance in the European case and the associated inequalities are not as strong as in the case of the countries that form MERCOSUR. Consequently, it would be most interesting to analyse and speculate on how the MERCOSUR financial union would take place in terms of the association between the various national 'cores' and the segmentation, separation and disintegration of the various national 'peripheries', and thus attempt to ascertain the likely domestic regional impact of this new external institutional arrangement. In the case of MERCOSUR, banks and foreign investors have, in relation to the periphery countries, problems associated with access to information and confidence in the information they do have access to. This is, in great part, the idea that orthodoxy presents when analysing the recent crises in emerging markets, that is, the idea of herd behaviour.[8] In the case of peripheral countries, this notion is more problematic when one thinks of the base of information necessary to extend credit to the internal peripheral regions that in this case are sub-peripheral.

Another important issue highlighted by Kregel (1993) is the level of regulation of the various financial systems in a monetary union. As a monetary union assumes mobility of financial systems, it prefers to locate lower costs. With regulation as an implicit cost, there will be a tendency to search for places of lower regulation, and this will mean that the level of regulation will be determined for the regulation of the whole system, or that the financial system will take on a lower level of regulation. In either case, there will be more freedom for the system to contribute to the intensification of the vicious circles above mentioned.

It follows from the analysis so far that monetary unions can cause huge problems when undertaken in systems that contain higher levels of structural inequalities. As regards market mechanisms, a strong tendency towards financial concentration is expected in the core region and, consequently, a concentration of growth in this region. Nevertheless, in the context of globalization, the formation of economic blocs may be the best way of including countries in this global economy. In this sense, institutional mechanisms should be created in order to avoid this concentration tendency. However, this will not materialize through market mechanisms. This is especially true in Third World countries where there are several institutional gaps in financial arrangements, especially in relation to the funding side of the problem (Studart, 1995). Therefore, in these countries, the state, or the coordination among all the national states, has a fundamental role to play in creating institutions and financial mechanisms which make possible growth and integration among all the economies of the bloc.

2. THE FINANCIAL SYSTEMS OF BRAZIL AND ARGENTINA

In the first years of the Asunción Agreement, there was a significant increase in intra-regional trade. The main points for discussion were postponed for later negotiations. Financial integration has taken place since to a limited extent and on a rather informal basis. This was the consequence of the increase in intra-regional capital flows, especially concerning direct investment, which was made easier by privatization, structural reforms and the opening up of the economies. This, however, seems to have reached an end. The easiest questions were solved, but it was not possible to avoid heated discussions on the most awkward issues. The new international scenario with more intense limits to an international capital flows also affected the integration perspectives of the regions. This was especially true in the exchange rate crisis of the Brazilian economy, that originated a series of problems for MERCOSUR.

In this new environment, it is necessary to analyse how desirable further financial integration of the region might be. It is, in fact, the main aim of this part of the chapter to examine the financial structure of the larger partners of MERCOSUR, analysing their similarities and differences. It will speculate on the possibility of reaching a monetary union and on the distributive impacts of this option. The data analyse aspects such as size, concentration and origin of capital, and some figures on monetary and financial data, productivity and regionalization.

2.1 Size and Concentration

There are two main segments of institutions in the Brazilian financial system: banking and non-banking institutions. In the first case, which is the main concern of this chapter, are the commercial banks, the *caixas econômicas*, credit cooperatives and universal banks. In December 1998, this segment claimed 1291 institutions, 203 banks, 173 universal, 28 commercial and 2 *caixas econômicas* – and 1088 credit cooperatives. The non-banking system comprised 612 institutions.

Its evolution, between 1993 and 1998, shows important changes at both the organizational and the operational level. There was a transfer of control, merger and liquidation, reducing the number of financial institutions (fewer credit cooperatives) to 24 per cent. If the investment funds, managers and special regimes are taken into account, the total number goes from 3348 to 6027 institutions, an increase of 80 per cent.

Some aspects of this system are interesting. In terms of size, the share of the national Brazilian system in the GDP, which was around 12 per cent to 15 per cent until 1994, decreased to around 7 per cent in 1995, as a consequence of the reduction of inflation. It is, in fact, a very concentrated banking system, with the largest banks representing 83 per cent of the total assets, and this tendency has been emphasized in the 1990s. The share of the ten largest banks is about 59 per cent in assets, 70 per cent in deposits, 60 per cent in net worth and 69 per cent of credit.

The banking system of Argentina, which had 124 banks in January 1999, presents the same tendency in terms of concentration and internationalization, varying only in intensity. It shows a larger share in the GDP, essentially because of its peculiarity in accepting loans and deposits in US dollars. However, it has a very tight concentration, measured by the participation of the tenth and twentieth largest banks (see Table 6.1).

2.2 Internationalization

The main difference in terms of internationalization is the origin of capital. In Argentina, internationalization, measured by access to the local market, is much greater than in Brazil. Foreign banks share 40 or 50 per cent of the net worth, deposits, loans and assets of the system, while private national banks do not have more than 18 or 20 per cent. The public sector controls just one-third of the system. In Brazil, the presence of the public sector is much bigger, followed by the national private sector. The foreign segment is still restricted to 8 or 15 per cent of the total system (see Table 6.2).

Even so, the foreign bank's strategy in the Brazilian market has been extremely aggressive in the last five years. Their participation doubled, in the main measures of the banking sector. The number of branches increased from 2 per cent (360) in 1995 to 15 per cent (2395) by the end of 1998. In access to foreign resources, a larger share of the international banks can be seen, increasing from 32 per cent to 46 per cent, with the reduction of the share of the national banks, which fell from 68 per cent in 1993, to 54 per cent in 1998. Still more important is their presence in the issue of bonds abroad and in the management of foreign investment funds in the domestic capital markets. Freitas et al. (1998) shows that in this broader perspective of foreign openness, which is not limited by presence in the national territory, internationalization is around 50 per cent (see Table 6.3) (Silva, 1998).

This internationalization process has several aspects. One of them has been analysed, though in an indirect way, as a consequence of the exchange crises which the emerging markets have been undergoing. The dollarization of the national liabilities produces even more fragility in the national financial systems. Their internationalization processes tend to make the use of foreign exchange in the domestic financial transactions easier.[9]

Another issue associated with the internationalization of the financial system which needs to be highlighted is the problem of credit creation in

Table 6.1 Argentina and Brazil: banking concentration (%)

	Loans		Deposits		Assets		Net worth	
	Argentina	Brazil	Argentina	Brazil	Argentina	Brazil	Argentina	Brazil
10 largest banks	64.5	68.7	62.8	70.5	60.0	59.2	64.3	60.4
20 largest banks	80.1	79.3	79.5	81.9	76.8	72.9	76.8	77.1

Source: Central Bank of Argentina and Central Bank of Brazil.

Table 6.2　Argentina and Brazil: financial system structure, December 1998 (share in the total, %)

	Public	Private	Private national	Private foreign
Argentina				
Net worth	38.9	61.1	19.2	41.9
Deposits	34.4	65.6	20.2	45.5
Loans	31.9	68.1	19.4	48.7
Assets	30.1	69.9	18.7	51.2
Brazil				
Net worth	36.8	63.2	48.8	14.4
Deposits	57.3	42.7	34.4	8.3
Loans	53.5	46.5	34.3	12.2
Assets	47.2	52.8	38.6	

Note:　The private banks category includes credit cooperatives and national banks with foreign participations.

Source:　Central Bank of Argentina and Central Bank of Brazil.

peripheral regions inside the countries analysed. As was previously demonstrated, there is a certain restriction related to the expectation formation and the remote character of these regions as related to the base of information. This makes the core more reluctant to extend loans to the periphery than periphery banks. When international banks are analysed, this process is emphasized, since in this case these regions are even more remote and the conventions, acting in a cumulative way, ration credit. In view of this, there would be a tendency towards greater regional disparities in financial systems that are deeply internationalized.

It can be said that, in the Brazilian case, the process of banking concentration in the 1990s was associated with a regional concentration process of the financial system. Since 1995, the national private banks with a regional character have almost disappeared. That is, the head offices of national and international banks were all concentrated in the Centre–South, and their action in the periphery was carried on only through the network of branches. This tends to create an extra financial constraint to these peripheral regions, given the more remote character of the information base of the core banks and the conventional basis of the decision-making process. At the same time, it can be seen that part of the restructuring of the financial sector has its basis on the action of banks in MERCOSUR (this, clearly, was the case of HSBC). Not only was it a process of loss of regional character and internationalization,

Table 6.3 Share of banks according to the origin of capital (%)

	Assets		Deposits		Credit operations		Worth	
	1994	1998	1994	1998	1994	1998	1994	1998
Foreign banks	7.1	14.2	4.6	8.3	5.2	12.2	9.6	14.4
Private national banks	41.2	38.1	39.3	33.7	35.4	33.3	55.6	47.2
Public banks	51.5	47.2	55.9	57.3	59.1	53.5	34.1	36.8
Credit cooperatives	0.2	0.5	0.2	0.7	0.3	1.0	0.7	1.6

Notes:
[a] Includes banks with foreign participation.
[b] Includes Bancodo Brasil Caixa Económica Federal and Caixas Estaduais.

Source: Central Bank, Semestral Report, Dec. 1998, Evolution of SFN.

from the internal point of view of Brazil, but also a process of solidification of the position of banks in MERCOSUR as a whole (Amado, 1997).

2.3   Financial and Monetary Aspects

On the macroeconomic level, Brazil has a more developed financial system than Argentina. The ratio of M1/GDP is smaller, but M3/GDP is larger, which is an indication of the more intense use of financial assets as a proportion of the GDP. This shows a more intense deepening of the financial system of Brazil, measured by the broader minus the narrower concepts of money in proportion to M3. In 1998 this ratio was 75.2 per cent in Argentina and 86 per cent in Brazil, as can be seen in Figures 6.1–6.7.

This may give Brazil some advantages in relation to Argentina in a financial integration process, since Brazilian assets tend to be more liquid. In terms of the capital account, there is a tendency for leakages from Argentina to Brazil, which puts Brazil in a better position. This would end up increasing the supply of liquidity in Brazil and reducing it in Argentina. As money is seen as a non-neutral element in our theoretical framework, this would end up in facilitating/accelerating growth in the Brazilian economy.

The use of cash also gives an indication of the development of the financial system. Chick and Dow (1996) refer to countries that use cash intensively for

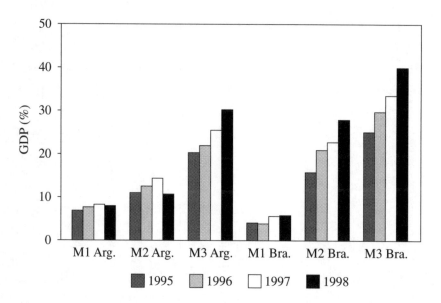

Figure 6.1   Argentina and Brazil: monetary indicators (% GDP)

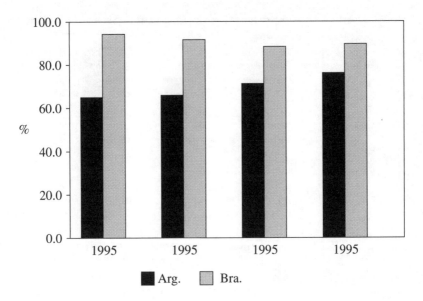

Figure 6.2   Argentina and Brazil: financial development (M3–M1)/M3

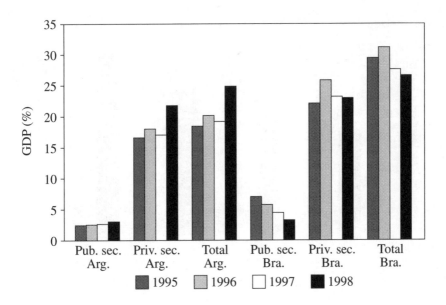

Figure 6.3   Argentina and Brazil: share of credit in GDP (%)

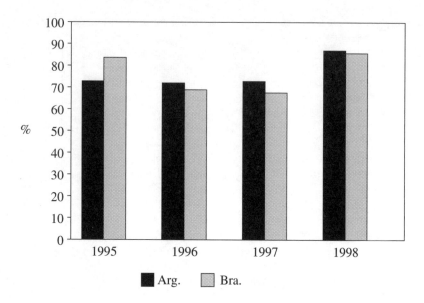

Figure 6.4   Argentina and Brazil: share of private credit in total credit (%)

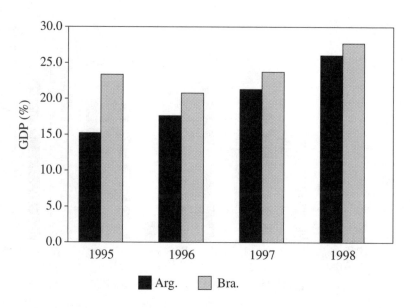

Figure 6.5   Argentina and Brazil: share of deposits in GDP (%)

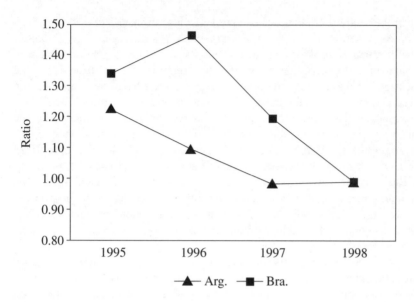

Figure 6.6   Argentina and Brazil: ratio of credit to deposits

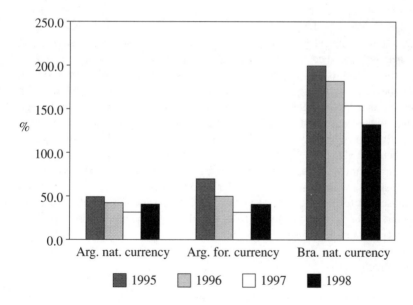

Figure 6.7   Argentina and Brazil: spread – percentage

their transactions as countries that are very close to stage 1 of banking development, where the deposit restriction on credit is still very evident. Countries that use mainly banking liabilities as money would be in stage 2 or more of banking development. Clearly, none of the countries that we are analysing are in stage 1. Consequently, the countries analysed here have overcome the stage where the focus is on the money multiplier and exogenous money. Therefore, the analysis that focuses on exogenous money supply has no relevance. The analysis, instead, is undertaken on the basis of an endogenous money supply. In Argentina, the cash/M1 ratio was 61 per cent and only 42 per cent in Brazil in 1998. This would give Brazil a relative advantage in its capacity for money creation by the banking system, and, again, show that the financial system has a more intense penetration in the Brazilian social fabric. In both cases, however, this ratio is still very high, which contrasts with the financial figures of both countries. Probably, the value of this ratio is associated with the exclusion characteristic of the financial system of these two countries, in both economic and social terms, in which a great part of the society is excluded from the financial system, thus needing to use cash to make their transactions.

Brazil, as previously mentioned, underwent an intensification of the internationalization process of the financial system after 1995. The official defence of this process was that the monetary stabilization process resulted in a fragile domestic financial system, unable to compete internationally. Moreover, the higher productivity of the international banks would create the conditions to reduce interest rates charged on loans for production and trade. However, a more focused analysis of the process shows a rapid convergence of the international banks to the 'tropical way' of conducting business, reducing the share of credit in their balance sheets, and increasing the share of their holdings of federal government bonds. Indeed, on certain occasions, they have been involved with speculative activities against the domestic currency. Data from ANDIMA, in Boechat and Melo (1999), confirm this contention, demonstrating that foreign banks, in the last trimester of 1997, earned the largest part of their income, of the magnitude of roughly 35 per cent, in operations with public debt financing.

There are also deep similarities in the recent trends of credit creation to the private sector (see Table 6.4). But there are large differences in terms of banking margins, which are much smaller in Argentina than Brazil, essentially because the former's financial system takes deposits and supplies loans in foreign currency. Again different from Brazil, Argentina has almost two-thirds of its credit and deposits in US dollars.[10]

2.4 Productivity

When figures like the number of employees per bank, the number of branches and accounts are analysed (see Table 6.5), it looks as if the banking system in

Table 6.4 Argentina and Brazil: credit operations and deposits, October 1998

	Public sector	$ local	$ foreign	Private sector	$ local	$ foreign	Total US$ millions	$ foreign (%)
Credit operations								
Argentina	7 820	1 806	6 014	66 527	24 622	41 905	74 347	64.5
Brazil	29 686	29 686	0	179 761	179 761	0	209 447	0.0
Deposits								
Argentina							76 396	66.0
Brazil							213 243[a]	0.0

Note: [a] Includes term deposits, time deposits and saving accounts.

Source: Mercosul – Basic Macroeconomic Indicators, no. 50, February 1999.

119

Table 6.5   Argentina and Brazil: banking productivity, January 1998

	Argentina	Brazil
Private banks		
Employees per bank	537	1 346
Employees per branch	24.5	30.3
Accounts per employee	122.5	88.9
Public banks		
Employees per bank	2 351	11 802
Employees per branch	31.3	34.6
Accounts per employee	71.7	59.4
Total		
Employees per bank	788	2 621
Employees per branch	26.9	32.5
Accounts per employee	101.5	72.7

Source: Central Bank of Argentina and Central Bank of Brazil.

Argentina is much more productive than that in Brazil. This may reflect the degree of internationalization and the kind of services available in each banking system, with Brazil showing broader availability.

2.5   Regional Considerations

The analysis of the regional aspects of the financial system is extremely important for the purposes of this chapter. As was suggested earlier, monetary union is the last step in the direction of transforming national economies to regional economies, at least at the economic level. It is, thus, possible to assume a central system and a peripheral system inside an economic bloc and attempt to establish a tendency towards convergent or divergent patterns of development among these systems. Market mechanisms, when acting within different economic and financial structures, tend to deepen the original inequalities, and, thus, increase the gap of development. In the case we are analysing, it seems clear that the process of integration among the two countries, which is under way as a consequence of the internationalization of both financial systems, has its basis on the integration of the two core regions of the two countries. Therefore, there is a tendency to form a supranational core region. The danger with this development is that peripheral regions may not have access to the 'new' financial system (Amado, 1997).

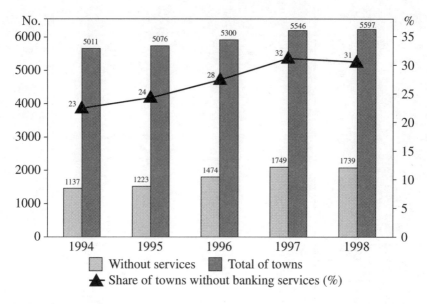

Figure 6.8   Brazil: towns without banking services

This tendency can be observed with the coincidence of the increase in the number of towns that have no supply of financial services in the Brazilian economy (see Figure 6.8). This has taken place in an economy where the degree of internationalization of the national financial system intensified after 1995. Ironically, this seems to be one of the important variables that explain the reduction of the access in the peripheral towns to the banking network in Brazil. In 1994 there were 1137 (23 per cent of total towns) towns without any banking services, and in 1998 this number grew to an unbelievable 17 399 (31 per cent of total towns).

We now turn to the level of concentration of the banking system in Argentina and Brazil (Table 6.6). Argentina presents a more regionally concentrated financial system, which is especially true when the three largest states are observed. However, these data should be analysed carefully in order to isolate the problem of concentration of population. This exercise reveals that Argentina presents a relatively less concentrated financial system than Brazil. The larger level of concentration in Argentina is the result of a population that is more concentrated in spatial terms, and is not only due to the financial concentration. The relatively lower financial concentration of Argentina is reflected in the larger presence of banking services at the national level, where there is a branch of banks for every 6500 inhabitants, while in Brazil this ratio is one branch for every 9400 inhabitants. This makes a difference in the

Table 6.6 Argentina and Brazil: regional concentration of the financial system, December 1998

	Branch offices, no.	Deposits, US$ millions	Population, 000s	Deposits/ branch, US$ millions	Population/ branch	Deposits/ population US$
Argentina						
3 largest provinces	3 183	64 483	18 327	20	5 758	3 518
5 largest provinces	3 929	68 862	22 538	18	5 736	3 055
10 largest provinces	4 426	72 303	25 824	16	5 835	2 800
Total	5 028	77 670	32 599	15	6 483	2 383
3 largest/total (%)	63.3	83.0	56.2			
5 largest/total (%)	78.1	88.7	69.1			
10 largest/total (%)	88.0	93.1	79.2			
Brazil						
3 largest states	8 280	221 218	61 905	27	7 476	3 574
5 largest states	10 872	256 323	79 862	24	7 346	3 210
10 largest states	13 675	289 330	114 667	21	8 385	2 523
Total	16 060	305 998	150 689	19	9 383	2 031
3 largest/total (%)	51.6	72.3	41.1			
5 largest/total (%)	67.7	83.8	53.0			
10 largest/total (%)	85.1	94.6	76.1			

Source: Central Bank of Argentina and Central Bank of Brazil.

deposit/branch ratio, which is larger in Brazil: US$19 million in Brazil and US$15 million in Argentina. The ratio deposit/population presents very similar figures, varying in the range US$2000–3500.

Both systems, however, present an extremely concentrated banking system, which generates a tendency to exclude the peripheral regions from the possible benefits of a financial integration process. Moreover, the integration can intensify the financial concentration due to endogenous mechanisms that tend to redirect the creation of liquidity towards the core regions, given the comparative advantage enjoyed by the financial system of these regions.

3.   SUMMARY AND CONCLUSIONS

There are several approaches to the regional integration question. One option is the neoliberal perspective, which assumes market-friendly policies that tend to lead the economy to external disequilibria, characterized by dependence on foreign short-term capital. According to this approach, it does not matter if globalization is a movement towards international integration, privately and informally led, and not taking into account local peculiarities as well as local and public interest (Vieira, 1999). It is seen as an unavoidable process. Zahler and Budnevich (1998) point out some necessary conditions for the emergence of regional integration: commitment to macroeconomic stability; macroeconomic coordination; banking supervision and regulation, with the creation of prudential criteria and so on.

MERCOSUR manifests several elements of this perspective, especially as a consequence of the position of its more open countries: Argentina, Paraguay and Uruguay. However, some of the assumptions of this model have not been accepted. For instance, the process is supposed to be continued; it is also assumed that the more advanced regulation should prevail, which is not what has been happening in this specific case.

The development and deepening of the integration in the financial sphere depends only on the external equilibrium of the region, since integration is seen as something positive for the economies of the regions. Therefore, it should be intensified and its velocity should be increased. This may be the reason for the insistence on the monetary integration of the area by Argentina, a proposal that has recently been substituted by the dollarization of the whole region.

On the other hand, it can be thought of as a model where the integration process is built from inside the countries and their specificities are respected (Vieira, 1999; Ferrer, 1997). This is also compatible with the Post-Keynesian perspective, which emphasizes the differences in economic structures, showing that these differences may generate vicious circles that can deepen the gap of development among the countries/regions involved in the process of integration. This is especially true when financial liberalization is pursued by a process of opening up of the capital account of the countries concerned.

In the case of MERCOSUR, the internationalization of the financial systems, instead of intensifying the supply of finance to the productive sector, where the higher productivity of the international banks could contribute to the growth process, has instead increased the vulnerability of these countries with respect to foreign exchange crises. Another important issue is the tendency towards banking concentration and the consequent tendency to increase regional disparities. These impacts depend on the larger or smaller degree of original inequalities in the whole system both inside and among the countries involved in the process.

As a result of all these considerations, MERCOSUR runs the risk of not being in a process of integration in the sense of Vieira (1999). The idea is that an area of economic integration should reflect not only the level of integration already reached but should also point to the joint desire of going ahead with deepening the process of integration. In this sense, the lack of development and intensification of integration inside the bloc, and the emphasis on negotiations with other countries, show a certain degree of slowing down of the whole process.

We may conclude by suggesting that the relevant matter is to know how the financial integration will proceed in terms of the association of several national centres and the disintegration of several national peripheries. All this is taking place in an environment of free international movement of capital, where the problem of uncertainty is extremely serious. Therefore, the role of the national states in this context of integration should be one of creating institutions and financial mechanisms that contribute to growth, in order to avoid further problems associated with the vulnerability of these countries in the new international scenario. Some examples along these lines include: financial devices that support investment in the infrastructure necessary for integration; cooperation among central banks to support payments using local currency, and macroeconomic cooperation that creates mechanisms to allow structural convergence among the economies that are under the same process of economic integration.

NOTES

*   A different version of this paper was published in *Estudos Econômicos*, Vol. 30, No. 4.
1.   The formation of these blocs enhanced the transactions within them, and reduced the transactions outside the bloc. This can lead to the wrong conclusion that regional integration erects barriers to the globalization process (Kleinknecht and Wengel, 1998). However, what seems more plausible is that both phenomena make a unique process, where globalization and regionalism interact and mutually intensify their depth.

2. For details on the European EMU see Barrel (1992), Britton and Mayes (1992), Caravelis (1996), Panic (1992), Ray and Whitley (1992) and Torres and Giovazzi (1993).
3. The viability of MERCOSUR has been jeopardized mainly as a consequence of the exchange rate crises across the international economy, and more specifically by the 1999 Brazilian crisis.
4. See on this point Giambiagi (1997, 1998) and comments in the *Gazeta Mercantil*, 15 April 1997, p. B2; also on the Argentinian attempt to harmonize the action of central banks, in *Folha de São Paulo*, 1 April 1997, p. 2. For discussion on the financial aspects of MERCOSUR, see *Folha de São Paulo*, Dinheiro, 12 January 1997. On the proposal for the monetary unification of MERCOSUR, see *Gazeta Mercantil*, 29 April 1997, p. A-11. The recent Brazilian crisis raises doubts about the possibilities discussed in the references just cited. Although what is discussed nowadays is still monetary unification, this is on the notion of currency boards in which the American dollar would be the monetary standard of MERCOSUR.
5. This literature analyses the problems associated with monetary integration. It shows that when there is no factor mobility and no fiscal coordination, there is no case for an optimal currency area.
6. There is analysis on these issues, but it tends to be mainly concerned with the European EMU.
7. This position, nevertheless, is not consensual. Davidson (1992) points out the advantages of the UMS (Unionized Monetary System) as a way of reducing the uncertainty associated with the exchange rate, but does not mention the vicious circle that the UMS can generate. When he unravels problems associated with monetary unions, he suggests that those problems can be avoided via fiscal transfers between the various countries that form the UMS.
8. This notion differs in a fundamental way from the kind of decision-making process analysed by Keynes. This is so because it assumes an ergodic environment in which the problem is associated with the capacity and access of agents to the base of information. That is why herd behaviour ends up being considered an irrational behaviour, which is the opposite conclusion from that reached by Keynes's analysis.
9. This is one of the explanations given by Calvo and Mendoza (1996) to the Mexican crisis.
10. It should be emphasized that this leaves Argentina in a much more fragile position than Brazil.

REFERENCES

Amado, A.M. (1997), *Disparate Regional Development in Brazil: A Monetary Production Approach*, Aldershot: Ashgate.

Amado, A.M. (1998), Impactos Regionais do Recente Processo do Processo de Concentração Bancária no Brasil, *Proceedings of the II Encontro Nacional de Economia Política,* Niterói, Brazil

Banco Central do Brasil (1998), *Evolução do Sistema Financeiro Nacional*, Relatório Semestral, December, Brazil.

Barrel, R. (ed.) (1992), *Economic Convergence and Monetary Union in Europe*, London: Sage.

Boechat, D. and Melo, E.L. (1999), *Maior Concentração e Participação do Capital Estrangeiro Caracterizam o SFN*, ANDIMA (internal discussion paper), São Paulo, Brazil.

Britton, A. and Mayes, D. (eds) (1992), *Achieving Monetary Union in Europe*, London: Sage.

Calvo, G.A. and Mendoza, E.G. (1996), Mexico's Balance-of-Payments Crises: A Chronicle of a Death Foretold, *Journal of International Economics*, Vol. 41, pp. 235–64.

Caravelis, G. (1996), *European Monetary Union: An Application of the Fundamental Principles*, Aldershot: Avebury.

Carvalho, F.C. (1997a), A Internacionalização do Setor Bancário Brasileiro, *Boletim de Conjuntura* IEI/UFRJ, Vol. 17, No. 3, pp. 21–34.

Carvalho, F.C. (1997b), Financial Innovation and Post Keynesian Approach to the 'Process of Capital Formation', *Journal of Post Keynesian Economics*, Vol. 19, No. 3, pp. 461–87.

Chick, V. and Dow, S.C. (1988), A Post-Keynesian Perspective on the Relation Between Banking and Regional Development, in P. Arestis (ed.), *Post Keynesian Monetary Economics*, Aldershot, UK and Brookfield, US: Edward Elgar, pp. 219–50.

Chick, V. and Dow, S.C. (1994), Competition and the Futures of the European Banking and Financial System, *Discussion Paper* No. 94–16, University College, London.

Chick, V. and Dow, S.C. (1996), Regulation and Differences in Financial Institutions, *Journal of Economic Issues*, Vol. XXX, No. 2, pp. 517–23.

Davidson, P. (1992), *International Money and the Real World*, New York: St. Martin's Press.

Dow, S. (1982), The Regional Composition of the Money Multiplier Process, *Scottish Journal of Political Economy*, Vol. 29, No. 1, pp. 22–44.

Dow, S. (1985), *Macroeconomic Thought: A Methodological Approach*, Oxford: Blackwell.

Dow, S. (1987), The Treatment of Money in Regional Economics, *Journal of Regional Science*, Vol. 27, No .1, pp. 13–34.

Dow, S. (1990), *Financial Markets and Regional Economic Development: The Canadian Experience*, Aldershot: Avebury.

Ferrer, A. (1997), Mercosul: Entre o Consenso de Washington e a Integração Sustentável, *RCBE* 51, April/June, pp. 40–52.

Folha de São Paulo (1997), issues of 11 January and 1 April.

Freitas, M.C.P. et al. (1998), *Abertura Externa e Sistema Financeiro*, IPEA/FUNDAP (internal discussion paper), São Paulo, May.

Gazeta Mercantil (1997), issue of 29 April.

Giambiagi, F. (1997), Unificação Monetária nos Países do Mercosul, *Revista de Economia Política*, Vol. 17, No. 4, pp. 5–31.

Giambiagi, F. (1998), *Moeda Única do Mercosul* (internal discussion paper).

Kleinknecht, A. and Wengel, J.T. (1998), The Myth of Economic Globalisation, *Cambridge Journal of Economics*, Vol. 22, pp. 637–47.

Kregel, J.A. (1993), Bank Supervision: The Real Hurdle to European Monetary Union, *Journal of Economic Issues*, Vol. XXVII, No. 2, pp. 667–76.

Mundell, R. (1961), A Theory of Optimal Currency Areas, *American Economic Review*, pp. 657–65.

Panic, M.C. (1992), *European Monetary Union: Lessons from the Classical Gold Standard*, London: Macmillan.

Plihon, D. (1995), A Ascensão das Finanças Especulativas, *Economia e Sociedade*, No. 5, pp. 61–79.

Ray, B. and Whitley, J. (eds) (1992), *Macroeconomic Policy Coordination in Europe: ERM and Monetary Union*, London: Sage.

Silva, L.A.S.A. (1998), Internacionalização do Sistema Financeiro Brasileiro na Década de Noventa, *Série Necema*, UnB, Brasília.

Studart, R. (1995), *Investment Finance in Economic Development*, London: Routledge.

Torres, F. and Giovazzi, F. (1993), *Adjustment and Growth in the European Monetary Union*, Cambridge: Cambridge University Press.

Vieira, J.L. (1999), As Bases Conceituais da Integração Econômica e do investimento Internacional no Mercosul: Fundamentos para Uma Revisão, unpublished PhD thesis, Department of Law, Universidade de São Paulo.

Zahler, R. and Budnevich, C. (1998), *Integracion Financiera Y Macroeconómica en El MERCOSUR*, Proceedings of the seminar on Policy Coordination in MERCOSUR, Buenos Aires.

PART III

Exchange Rate Regimes and Monetary
Dilemmas for MERCOSUR

7. Financial opening, instability and macroeconomic performance in Latin America during the 1990s: some possible perverse links

Rogério Studart[1]

1. INTRODUCTION

In the second half of the 1980s and throughout the first half of the 1990s, there was a spectacular growth of financial markets in the developed economies. This growth was soon followed by a significant surge of capital flows from mature economies to developing countries. In particular, in Latin America the opening of capital account (in the context of liberalizing policies of the end of 1980s and beginning of the 1990s) led to a very significant surge of voluntary foreign capital inflows.

In this chapter we claim that this surge had strong destabilizing effects on key economic variables, such as exchange rates, domestic supply of credit and domestic asset prices – soon followed by significant macro and financial imbalances. These in turn increased the vulnerability of Latin American economies to the shifts in the direction of capital flows. Furthermore, we claim that to a significant extent the abrupt and careless integration of two financial markets of quite distinct structure, size, depth and pace of growth originated this instability.

The chapter is structured in four parts in addition to this introduction. Section 2 contrasts the distinct structural features of financial systems of developed and Latin American economies in the 1980s. Section 3 presents a theoretical discussion of the possible transmission channels of surges of capital inflows into a bank-based developing economy. Section 4 builds on the analysis developed in sections 2 and 3 to assess the impacts of the surges of capital flows on macroeconomic performance and financial stability in the region. Section 5 presents some concluding remarks.

2. FINANCIAL SYSTEMS IN DEVELOPED ECONOMIES AND IN LATIN AMERICA IN THE 1990S

Financial systems in a number of key mature economies (especially the USA) changed dramatically in the 1980s and 1990s, as a consequence of domestic deregulation and external financial liberalization.[2] At least four strong trends are observed.

First, a well-known process of disintermediation occurred: the traditional banking institutions were transformed into new financial services firms – including those of institutional securities firms, insurance companies and asset managers. In addition non-bank financial institutions – such as mutual funds, investment banks, pension funds and insurance companies – began actively competing with banks both on the asset and liability sides of banks' balance sheets. Second, the deregulation and growth of institutional investors – in special pension funds and insurance companies – have made their role in the provision of loanable funds more prominent. Finally, external liberalization and significant improvements in information technology have increased across-the-border dealings of securities, and internationalization of the financial business.

The mere fact that new financially 'heavyweight' agents (investment banks, mutual funds and institutional investors) were allowed to expand their securities trading led to a rapid growth of prices in the secondary markets. This created a virtuous circle of expansion of asset prices and markets: as financial wealth increased, investors' expectations were fulfilled, leading to further rounds of financial investment. Not surprisingly, the total financial assets in the hands of institutional investors more than doubled from 1987 to 1990, and almost doubled from 1990 to 1996 (Table 7.1).

Table 7.1   Financial assets in the hands of institutional investors in selected OECD economies, 1987–96

	1987	1990	1993	1996
USA	3471	5461	7946	11343
Japan	576	1403	2075	2376
Germany	219	525	578	881
France	278	618	847	1111
United Kingdom	482	1080	1480	1877
Other OECD	628	1361	1830	2327
Total	5654	10448	14756	19915

Source: BIS (1998: 76–97). Data consolidated by the author.

In addition, as evidenced by Fornari and Levy (1999), the gross financial assets of the G6 doubled as a proportion of GDP between 1980 and 1994, whereas the liquidity of these assets increased substantially.[3] Just to give a measure of this trend, from 1989 to 1993, the outstanding amounts of debt securities issued in OECD economies increased over US$6 trillion, and more than doubled from 1989 to 2000 (Table 7.2).

In contrast to what happened in developed economies, and as in most developing economies (Beck et al., 2000), Latin American financial systems in the early 1990s continued to suffer from the similar three structural problems described by Raymond Goldsmith (1969) in the 1960s. First, the banking sector is relatively small, including the refinancing of government debt, whereas spreads charged by the banking sector are still much higher than those found in developed economies.[4]

Second, the supply of finance is still very short term as well as rationed to specific sectors. Third, as indicated by Figure 7.1, securities markets are small and very concentrated.

Given the differences in terms of the depth and of the pace of expansion of financial markets in developed and Latin American economies, the association between capital account and financial liberalization was likely to be destabilizing – as we shall discuss below.

3. THE CONSEQUENCES OF FINANCIAL INTEGRATION OF UNEVEN PARTNERS: A THEORETICAL ASSESSMENT

Surges of financial flows affect domestic macroeconomic performance depending on at least four factors: (a) the 'international financial environment', as defined by the degree of mobility of capital between developed and developing economies, the volume of flows relative to the size of the economy and their volatility; (b) the policy (exchange rate, trade, monetary and fiscal) regimes adopted by the developing economy; (c) specific domestic factors, such as the size, development and depth of domestic financial institutions and markets, and the growth dynamics before and during the surge of capital flows; (d) the soundness of domestic financial institutions, which depend both on the quality of regulation and supervision and on macroeconomic variables.

3.1(a) The International Financial Environment and the Policy Regimes Adopted by Latin American Economies in the 1990s

As regards the international financial environment (IFE hereafter) the deregulation of capital accounts in both developed and developing economies

Table 7.2 Outstanding amounts of debt securities issued in domestic markets, 1989–2000 (US$ billions and %)

Year	1989	1993	1997	2000	1989	1993	1997	2000
	US$ Billions				% of total			
All issuers	14042	20565	25464	29733	100.0	100.0	100.0	100.0
OECD	13559	19967	24452	28580	96.9	97.1	96.0	96.1
USA	6682.8	9226.7	12059	14545.9	47.6	44.9	47.4	48.9
Japan	2626.7	4010.1	4399.3	6072.3	18.7	19.5	17.3	20.4
France	557.6	995.7	1102.5	1068.1	4.0	4.8	4.3	3.6
Germany	668.4	1458.4	1732.1	1711.6	4.8	7.1	6.8	5.8
UK	332.9	446.1	777.7	895.9	2.4	2.2	3.1	3.0
Latin America	172.1	296.7	490.6	482.8	1.2	1.4	1.9	1.6
Argentina	113.5	39	70.1	85.2	0.8	0.2	0.3	0.3
Brazil	n/a	189.9	344.5	292.5	n/a	0.9	1.4	1.0

Source: BIS database (www.bis.org); consolidated and elaborated by the author.

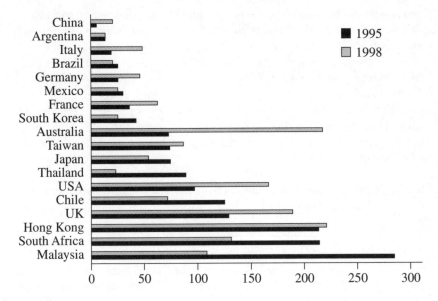

Source: International Finance Corporation.

Figure 7.1   Stock exchange capitalization as a share of GDP (%)

allowed for a significant increase in the volume and types of flows (particularly the expansion of portfolio flows). As already mentioned, given the depth
and pace of expansion of securities markets in developed economies, the relative size of capital flows *vis-à-vis* the size of the economy was significant.

In this context, excessive capital flows (in relation to the needs to finance
current account deficits) often led to excess supply of foreign reserves in the
economy, which creates pressure either to revalue the domestic currency or to
expand domestic liquidity – depending on the policy regimes adopted. Indeed,
policy regimes can be seen as the 'filters' in the transmission mechanisms of
surges of capital inflows, for at least three reasons. First, the capital account
regime can partly restrict the volume and the type of flows allowed into the
country.

Second, exchange rate regimes (ERRs) determine how excessive flows of
foreign capital are internalized. In a purely floating ERR, the impact of surges
would only fall on the exchange rate; that is, the excess would be translated
into exchange rate revaluation. In turn, in a pegged ERR, the surges will result
in expansion of domestic liquidity, even if the monetary authorities attempt to
sterilize it (more on this below). Third, monetary policy regimes determine
whether domestic monetary authorities will be prepared to sterilize or not the

additional liquidity created by a surge of capital flows. If the monetary authorities decide (or are able[5]) to sterilize, open market operations can keep interest rates high. It is important to note though, that in that case this will create
further incentives for continued capital inflows, as well as put pressure on
fiscal balance (more on this below).

Two other specific domestic characteristics of most developing countries
must be considered for a complete picture on the destabilizing effects of rapid
financial integration: the characteristics of the financial systems and the financial fragility at the moment when the surge of foreign capital flows begin.
These are discussed below.

3.1(b)   Characteristics of Financial Systems and the Internalization of Financial Flows

The shallowness of secondary asset markets in developing economies (Figure
7.1) makes domestic asset markets very sensitive to abrupt changes in liquidity. Unlike the situation in the US economy, the links between secondary and
primary securities markets are weak, so that a rapid expansion of the former
does not lead necessarily to an expansion in the issues of securities. To the
contrary, a rapid growth of the liquidity of these markets tends to become
mainly speculative bubbles, which create disincentives for both issuers and
long-term investors to remain in the market.[6]

A different logic applies to foreign direct investment (FDI) in the 1990s:
most FDI to developing economies has been associated with a process of
acquisitions of companies in the context of privatization of public companies
and banks. Of course these flows *per se* are only changes of ownership of capital, and do not lead to expansion of aggregate demand. But they do tend to
create rapid increases in share prices.

Even though securities markets are small, and their impact can be reduced
in affecting expenditure decisions, the burst of speculative bubbles can affect
both key domestic financial players and expectations in the economy. In both
cases, this can affect macroeconomic performance.

The structure of the credit market in Latin America also affects the way
foreign financial flows are internalized and their final macroeconomic effect.
Due to their balance sheet structure, banks are usually suppliers of short-term
credit. The shallowness of markets for long-term securities and the poor development of inter-bank deposit markets reduce their capacity to manage their
liabilities in order to compensate for changes in their reserves. In these circumstances, banks tend to be very conservative: they lend short, restrict lending to
privileged agents (large corporations and governments) and maintain high
spreads.

The access to international markets provides banks with expanded sources of funding at low interest rates (*vis-à-vis* domestic markets) and longer maturities. As long as the exchange rate is perceived as stable (as was the case in most economies in the region in the early 1990s), it is microeconomically rational to borrow long abroad to lend short domestically. Such an increase of external funding increases the domestic competition for expansion of bank loans.

The supply and maturities of loanable funds represent a constraint on the expenditure decision of different agents in the economy, being a more determined factor for some (for instance, consumers) than for others (for example, firms and governments). Surges of financial flows tend to reduce these constraints, as the additional domestic liquidity created by the domestic intermediation pushes domestic intermediaries to expand their assets. But final distribution of these loanable funds depends on the dynamics of growth; that is, for instance, the domestic economy in the early stages of the surge of capital flows is investment-led or consumption-led.[7]

In addition, given the same uncertainties and other characteristics of the financial sector, and as mentioned above, the intermediation spreads of even short-term credit tend to be very high, whereas the private supply of long-term loanable funds is simply irrelevant. All these supply and demand factors in the credit market in Latin America tend to create a significant causal relation between surges of financial flows, credit expansion and domestic consumption boom. These, in turn, affect financial stability, according to the inherited stage of financial fragility.

3.1(c)   The Soundness of Domestic Financial Institutions

A market economy is characterized by the fact that some expenditures (for instance, the acquisition of durable goods) and long-term uncertain undertakings (fixed capital, for instance) need to be financed via the issuance of short-term assets (such as bank deposits) or liquid marketable assets. This combination of uncertainty and maturity mismatching makes our economies inherently financially fragile.[8]

In general, though, periods of surges of capital flows are associated with improved expectations, both of international investors and domestic players, on the future macroeconomic performance of the economy. It is seemingly rational to assume that domestic bankers' expectations also tend to improve in such periods. In addition, in economies that adopt strong forms of pegged systems (such as in the Argentine currency board), the expansion of credit is likely to be associated with increasing currency mismatches.

That is, surges of capital flows tend to increase maturity and currency mismatches – and thus financial fragility. Fragility does not mean instability: it takes abrupt changes of certain key variables – for instance, an economic downturn, an abrupt change of interest rates and/or of the exchange rates (if a significant part of domestic liabilities are denominated in foreign currencies) – to turn financial fragility into financial instability.

Given the characteristics of developing markets described above, the policy regimes adopted in Latin America in the 1980s, and the analysis offered in the previous paragraph, how did large surges of financial flows affect domestic macroeconomic performance and financial stability? This is the theme of our last topic before the conclusion.

4. SURGES OF FOREIGN CAPITAL INFLOWS, MACROECONOMIC PERFORMANCE AND DOMESTIC FINANCIAL STABILITY

As mentioned above, the first half of the 1990s was characterized by a surge of capital flows to developing countries. As indicated by Table 7.3, these flows have only been a fraction of those between mature economies, but by all measures are significant *vis-à-vis* the size of developing economies and their domestic financial markets.[9]

The policy regimes in many Latin American economies had some distinctive features, but were also in a certain way 'influenced' by the opportunity offered by such an excessive supply of foreign capital. After one decade of balance-of-payments constraints (and net negative resource transfers), leading to very poor macroeconomic performance and high inflation in Latin America, the surge of capital inflows *cum* trade liberalization eased the external constraint for the expansion of domestic demand associated with expanding imports.[10]

Thus, for a significant number of Latin American economies, the policy regime adopted in the early 1990s was a mixture of highly liberal capital account and trade policies – with an important exception, that is Chile, where some policies towards selective entry of capital were implemented. Exchange rate policies were used as anchors for price stabilization policies, whereas the monetary policy maintained the differentials between domestic and international interest rates high enough to continue attracting capital flows (and particularly portfolio flows).

How did the domestic financial systems react to this environment?

4.1 Credit Expansion and Consumption-led Growth

Surges of foreign capital flows to Latin America are often associated with the expansion of domestic credit (Figure 7.2), higher leverage of domestic banks and higher levels of indebtedness by private and public agents.

Table 7.3 Developing country shares, 1991–2000 (percentages except where stated otherwise)

	1991	1992	1993	1994	1995	1996	1997	1998	1999	2000
In global total private capital flows	11.8	12.4	12.6	12.8	12.4	13.2	14.4	9.9	7.6	7.6
In global output	19.8	19.2	19.7	20	20.7	22.1	23.2	21.6	21.7	22.5
In global trade	26.5	28.3	28.3	28.4	29.5	31.3	32.4	30.7	30.7	33.4
In global population	84.1	84.3	84.4	84.5	84.6	84.7	84.9	85	85.1	85.2
Memo items (billions of dollars)										
Global capital market flows	794	850	1226	1501	1928	2403	2929	3033	3910	4324
Global FDI	160	172	226	256	331	377	473	683	982	1118

Source: World Bank (2001).

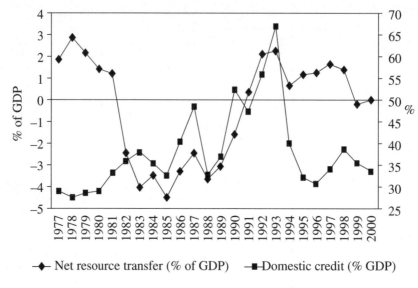

Source: UN/ECLAC (2002).

Figure 7.2   Latin America: net resources transfers and domestic credit, 1977–2000 (% GDP)

As expected, the way this additional credit was allocated was directly affected by the growth dynamics before the surge of foreign capital inflows. In Latin America, long-term expectations, and thus investment, tended to be highly depressed in the 1980s. And given the macroeconomic uncertainties and the extent of competitive pressure put on investors, it also tended to be depressed in the 1990s.

If investment did not react rapidly to the surge of capital inflows, consumption did. The reason is again financial: consumer credit in the region, due to the characteristics of the domestic financial structure mentioned below, is highly rationed. In contrast with investment, thus consumption responded rapidly to changes in the supply of credit. In contrast, in some East Asian economies, for instance, the surge of capital inflows was associated with expansion of investment (see, for example, Park, 1998). This is not at all surprising given that one of the characteristics of the region in the recent past was a sustained growth led by domestic investment and exports and government deficits and debts were relatively small in the early 1990s. Thus in Latin America the surge of foreign capital flows was very much associated with 'overconsumption' – and, given the degree of trade liberalization, with increasing deficits in the trade account (more on this below).

Of course, the way the additional credit was allocated directly affected other variables, and particularly those that determined the external financial dependence and macroeconomic performance in the 1990s.

4.2 External Financial Dependence and Macroeconomic Performance

Using the excessive capital inflows to stabilize prices and to grow had two interrelated costs. First, as mentioned above, in Latin America the surge of foreign capital flows in the early 1990s was often associated with 'overconsumption', and despite the growth of exports, the trade and current accounts deteriorated almost continuously until 1998 – the exceptions between the two years after the tequila crisis (1994). This led to increasing needs for external financing and thus to higher external debts and the external debt services.

As external dependence grew, so did the constraints on domestic policy. First, in order to maintain the attractiveness for international investors and domestic borrowers, in many economies monetary policies started targeting

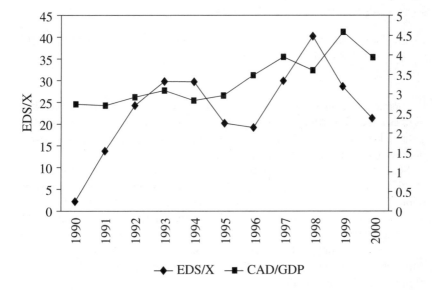

Source: UN/ECLAC (1992: 146).

Figure 7.3   *Two indicators of financial dependence and vulnerability of Latin American economies in the 1990s: current account balance/GDP (CAG/GDP) and external debt services/exports (EDS/X), 1990–2000 (%)*

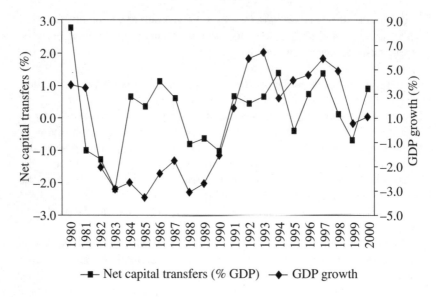

—■— Net capital transfers (% GDP)   —◆— GDP growth

Source: Author's construct based on data from ECLAC.

Figure 7.4   Latin America: net capital transfers (% GDP) and GDP growth, 1980–2000 (% annual average)

the maintenance of high interest differentials, whereas fiscal discipline was used as a tool for adding credibility for the stability of exchange rate regimes. Thus, attracting capital flows became a crusade that often included a policy package (beyond the exchange rate regime).[11]

Second, the combination of high levels of interest rates made the process of fiscal adjustment difficult and led to loss of international competitiveness of domestic corporations, low levels of economic activity and rising unemployment. Domestic economic cycles became highly dependent on the availability of foreign capital.

These two factors partly explain why in the 1990s economic cycles in Latin American economies moved in the same direction of capital flows to the region – as indicated by Figure 7.4.

4.3   Domestic Financial Fragility

On several occasions in the past (but more obviously in the 1990s), surges of capital flows in Latin America were also associated with domestic financial crises (mainly of the banking sector). These crises in turn prompted policies not only to avoid systemic effects, but also to restructure the domestic banking sector and improve prudential regulation and supervision.[12] The reasons for these crises vary, but certainly there are some important links with the abrupt process of financial integration of the 1990s.

First, the abrupt financial integration led to the overborrowing syndrome, to a rapid process of assets and liabilities dollarization and to volatile behaviour of prices of domestic securities and other real assets. The overborrowing syndrome[13] leads to increasing vulnerability of domestic borrowers to changes in international interest rates and exchange rates – a vulnerability that is related to the increasing currency mismatching.

Second, in the region, such a process took different forms and depths, according to the characteristics of the policy package adopted – but it did happen in a significant number of economies. In Argentina, for instance, there was a rapid increase of dollar-denominated contracts – particularly of consumer and corporate loans (Figure 7.5(a)). In contrast in Brazil, where law forbids private contracts denominated in foreign currency, asset dollarization took mainly the form of dollar-indexed government bonds – whereas the dollarization of banks' assets and liabilities remained limited (Figure 7.5(b)).[14]

Third, prices of domestic assets started moving in tandem with capital flows, and thus in a very volatile manner, whereas domestic primary markets shrank. This partly explains, for instance, the strong relation between net resources transfers and stock price indexes in Latin America in the 1990s.

In the region, securities markets, when they exist at all, are quite small and affect only marginally (through the formation of expectations, for instance) the macroeconomic performance.[15]

On the one hand this increasing volatility very probably affected domestic expectations. On the other hand, it created further incentives for large domestic corporations to issue securities abroad, the result being the financial integration of the 1990s which led to shrinkage of primary markets, associated both with the delisting of large companies and their option to issue securities abroad (Dowers et al., 2000). This in turn led to the expansion of private external debt – and thus higher currency mismatches and financial fragility of the economy.

Fourth, currency crises have become more frequent, often associated with rapid devaluation and/or interest rate hikes. In the context of high maturity and currency mismatches and/or increased financial leverage, raising the domestic interest rates or devaluing exchange rates is a recipe for financial instability[16] – as the experiences of Mexico in 1994 and Argentina in 2002 clearly indicate.

(a) Argentina

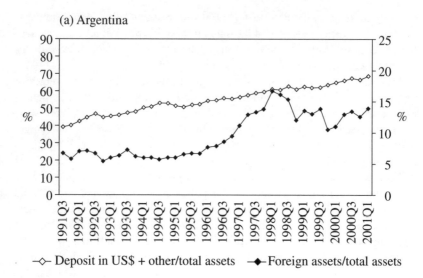

—◇— Deposit in US$ + other/total assets   —◆—Foreign assets/total assets

(b) Brazil

—■— Foreign liabilities/total assets   —□— Foreign assets/total assets

Source: Author's construct based on data from IMF, *International Financial Statistics.*

Figure 7.5   Argentina and Brazil: dollarization of the bank assets and liabilities, 1991Q3–2001Q1

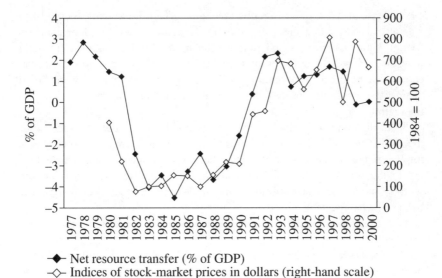

◆ Net resource transfer (% of GDP)
◇ Indices of stock-market prices in dollars (right-hand scale)

Source: UN/ECLAC (2002).

Figure 7.6 Latin America: net resources transfers (% GDP) and stock market index, 1977–2000

5. CONCLUDING REMARKS

The nature and the transmission of surges of foreign financial flows seem to have become quite different since the 1980s. Financial globalization not only means an increase of financial flows between developed and developing economies, but also deeper financial linkages between economic agents of these economies. This integration is inherently destabilizing due to the wide (and widening) differences between financial markets in mature and developing economies. Domestic policies in developing countries can mitigate, but not avoid, these destabilizing effects. These destabilizing effects are indeed in the heart of the macro and financial instabilities in Latin America in the 1990s.

In the first half of the 1990s the combination of stable (and sometimes overvalued) exchange rates, commercial opening and financial opening, and fiscal discipline led to a virtuous circle in which the rapid achievement of price stability and exchange rate overvaluation further attracted foreign capital inflows.

The virtuosity of this circle proved to be a double-edged sword in the second half of the 1990s, however, a feature that was already signalled by the

1994 Mexican crisis and the tequila contagion effect. From that experience, it was already clear that the economies in the region were too dependent on foreign financial inflows and thus on the moods of international financial investors. However, the prompt recovery of the flows to Latin American economies reduced the overall concerns, and very few voices were heard against the continuing process of external fragilization that was in course in the region.

From the eruption of the East Asian crisis in 1997–98, the deterioration of the confidence of foreign investors was reflected in increasing country risk implicit in the need to maintain even higher levels of interest rates. This in turn led to the widening financial disequilibria in domestic public and private sectors, while the disequilibria of the trade and services accounts of the balance of payments persisted.

Ultimately the growing emerging-market crisis hit the LAC region, beginning with the contagion of the East Asian financial crisis and culminated with the 1999 speculative attack on Brazil – an attack that led (initially) to a chaotic process of devaluation of the Brazilian real. The pressures on Brazil ceded and the price and output effects were far less drastic than expected (by the most optimistic analysts). Nevertheless the devaluation of the real brought a severe misalignment of exchange rates in some important partners of Brazil in the region, especially those in the MERCOSUR bloc. As occurred in East Asia, the pressures for competitive exchange devaluation became significant and further increased the policy constraints and challenges that are faced by the region now.

A process of competitive devaluation *per se* can have drastic effects on domestic prices and output – as the experience in Europe in the 1970s–1980s and, more recently, in East Asia indicate. In economies with low levels of domestic asset and liability dollarization, these effects tend to diminish with time, as real exchange levels are established around their equilibrium levels. However, due to the degree of dollarization of domestic assets and liabilities in countries such as Argentina, Paraguay and Uruguay – just to mention a few – devaluation tends to have further consequences for their domestic financial systems. And financial instability, as is well documented, tends to have long-term negative effects on macroeconomic performance and trade.

The 1990s experience is not the first traumatic experience of financial opening and liberalization, and it is unlikely to be the last. It is hoped that two lessons can be drawn from this traumatic experience. First, if MERCOSUR or any other trade bloc in the region is to be sustainable in the future, one crucial target should be to avoid such processes leading to financial vulnerability of the economies. Second, and as a consequence of the first lesson, the deregulation of the capital and financial account should always be very gradual, respecting the structural asymmetries that exist between financial systems of developed and developing economies.

NOTES

1. The views expressed herein are those of the author and do not necessarily reflect those of ECLAC.
2. For more detailed description of the changes in the financial systems of mature economies, see, *inter alia*, BIS (1986), Franklin (1993), Feeney (1994), Helleiner (1994), Bloomestein (1995) and Group of Ten (2001).
3. This process would probably end up in a traditional Minskian asset crisis (Minsky, 1982; Taylor and O'Connell, 1985), were it not for the characteristics of the financial markets in some mature economies – particularly the US financial markets. This characteristic has to do with the significant size and depth of securities markets and the strong link between secondary and primary markets. The result of this link was that the growth of capital markets provided new sources of finance to the corporate sector (for instance, the IT sector, 'dot.com' companies and so on), a trend that has been highly leveraged by the use of financial derivatives to unbundle risks and securitize. This provided the financing required for the technological revolution and productivity expansion that in turn permitted the astonishing growth of the US 'new economy' in the 1990s.
4. More on these structural features of financial systems in Latin America in section 3 below.
5. In an extreme case of fixed ERR, such as the Argentinean currency board, the option to sterilize is limited. In that case, constraints on the expansion of liquidity will have to be placed on the domestic banks' capacity to expand credit, for instance through higher reserve requirements. Indeed this was the option taken in Argentina, but also in the early stages of the Brazilian stabilization plan in 1994.
6. Furthermore, in the context of rapid financial integration and exchange rate stability, the larger size and greater depth of securities markets in mature economies makes it more attractive for large corporations (exactly those that issue securities in developing economies) to issue abroad. Paradoxically, thus, surges of capital flows in the context of the 'integration of uneven partners' tends to exacerbate the speculative nature of securities markets, and to create barriers to the long-term development of these markets in developing economies.
7. This partly explains why in Latin America, where investment had been very depressed in the 1980s, financial opening and integration in the 1990s often led to 'consumption booms'; whereas in East Asia, the same process led to ' over-investment'. More on this in the next section.
8. In an economy with developed financial asset markets, the changes in expectation of players in financial markets, which can be significant in periods of uncertainty, could lead to significant changes in the demand for money and interest rates (Keynes, 1936). This might not only create undesirable changes in relative prices of all other assets and goods, but also reduce productive entrepreneurs' capacity to repay their debts. Minsky (for example 1982), based on Fisher's (1933) early description of debt-deflation processes, showed that if monetary authorities did not intervene in this case, this process would lead to decline in output, employment and bankruptcies. If such a process of debt-deflation becomes a self-fulfilling prophecy, it will not be easily reversed by spontaneous means (Taylor and O'Connell, 1985). And it can create a path-dependent process: bankruptcies are irreversible changes, and if their number is significant, potential output is reduced and growth perspectives are lower. Rational long-term investors would have less confidence in such an economy, leading to lower investment and growth. The expectations that led to the debt-deflation process can become a long, persistent process of stagnation.
9. Even though country-specific features did affect the distribution of such flows between developing economies, the push factors, related to the changes in financial markets in developed economies, seem to be the most important factor in explaining such growth. This can be seen by the growth of flows to both Latin America and the Caribbean (LAC hereafter) in the 1980s and 1990s, two regions known to have significant macroeconomic performances and that none the less had similar trends of capital flows in the 1990s.
10. The surge of capital flows significantly surpassed the needs to finance both the current and the capital account, generating systematic accumulation of reserves in the region.

11. On this, see UN/ECLAC (2002: Ch. 5).
12. This is an important topic for several reasons: first, such processes often came with fiscal costs that made the maintenance of fiscal discipline even tougher; second, the restructuring of the banking system was normally associated with opening up the domestic financial sector to foreign investors; third, these regulatory and supervisory changes are affecting the way banks and other financial institutions intermediate loanable funds in the economy – a factor that is important for long-term growth perspectives of some of the economies. These topics go far beyond the scope of this chapter, but see, for instance, Stallings and Studart (2001) for a discussion of them.
13. That is, the expansion of external debt in excess of the need to finance current account deficits leading to accumulation of reserves in periods of surges of financial flows to the region.
14. For an analysis of the process of liability dollarization in the MERCOSUR region, see Studart and Hermann (2001).
15. An important exception is the Brazilian case, as is evidenced by Studart (1999).
16. And indeed there were many occasions when both had to be done in view of abrupt reversals of foreign capital flows.

REFERENCES

Beck, T.A. Demirgüç-Kunt, R. Levine and V. Maksimovic (2000), 'Financial Structure and Economic Development: Firm, Industry and Country Evidence', mimeo, in www.worldbank.org, August.
BIS (Bank for International Settlements) (1986), 'Recent Innovations in International Banking', mimeo, April.
BIS (1998), *68th Annual Report*, Basle, June.
Blommestein, H.J. (1995), 'Structural changes in financial markets: overview of trends and prospects', in OECD (1995), pp. 9–47.
Dowers, K., F. Gomez-Acebo and P. Masci (2000), 'Making capital markets viable in Latin America', *Infrastructure and Financial Markets Review*, Vol. 6, no. 3, Washington: IMF, December.
Feeney, P.W. (1994), *Securitization: Redefining the Bank*, The Money and Banking Series (gen. ed. John R. Presley), New York: St. Martin's Press.
Fisher, I. (1933), 'The debt-deflation theory of great depression', *Econometrica*, Vol. 1: 337–57.
Fornari, F. and A. Levy, (1999), 'Global liquidity in the 1990s: geographical and long run determinants', *BIS Conference Papers No. 8*, in www.bis.org/publ/confer08.htm.
Franklin, R.E. (1993), 'Financial Markets in Transition – or the Decline of Commercial Banking', in Federal Reserve Bank of Kansas: *Changing Capital Markets: Implications for Monetary Policy, Proceedings*, Jackson Hole, Wyoming, 19–21 August.
Goldsmith, R. (1969), *Financial Structure and Development*, New Haven: Yale University Press.
Group of Ten (2001), 'Report on Consolidation in the Financial Sector' (Basle: Group of Ten), in www.bis.org.
Helleiner, E. (1994). *States and the Re-emergence of Global Finance: From Bretton Woods to the 1990s*, Ithaca and London: Cornell University Press.
Keynes, J.M. (1936), *The General Theory of Employment, Interest and Money*, London: Macmillan, 1947.

Minsky, H.P. (1982), 'The financial-instability hypothesis: capitalist processes and the behaviour of the economy', in C.P. Kindleberger and J.P. Laffargue (eds), *Financial Crises*, Cambridge: Cambridge University Press.

Park, Y.C. (1998), 'The financial crisis in Korea and its lessons for reform of the international financial system', in J.J. Teunissen (ed.), *Regulatory and Supervisory Challenges in a New Era of Global Finance*, The Hague: FONDAD.

Stallings, B. and R. Studart (2001), 'Financial Regulation and Supervision in Emerging Markets: The Experience of Latin America since the Tequila Crisis', ECLAC, Economic Development Division, mimeo.

Studart, R. (1999), 'Pension funds and the financing of productive investment: an analysis based on Brazil's recent experience', *Série Financiamiento del Desarollo* 102, LC/L.1409-P.

Studart, R. and J. Hermann (2001), 'Sistemas financeiros no Mercosul: desenvolvimento recente e perspectivas de integração', in R. Baummann (ed.), *Avanços e Desafios da Integração*, Brasília: IPEA.

Taylor, Lance and Stephen A. O'Connell (1985), 'A Minsky Crisis,' *Quarterly Journal of Economics,* **100** (supp.), 871–86.

United Nations (1999), *World Economic and Social Survey*, New York: United Nations.

UN/ECLAC (United Nations/Economic Commission for Latin America and the Caribbean) (2002), *Globalization and Development*, Santiago, Chile: UN/ECLAC.

World Bank (2001), *Global Development Finance*, Washington, DC: World Bank.

8. Monetary dilemmas: Argentina in MERCOSUR

José Maria Fanelli and Daniel Heymann[*]

1. INTRODUCTION

The Argentine economy was known during decades for its high and stubborn inflation. Price instability reached a climax in several bursts of hyperinflation, which severely disturbed even day-to-day transactions. In the 1990s, the country adopted a strict system of convertibility with a hard peg to the dollar. Under this system, inflation definitely stopped. The economy initially experienced a spending boom, and managed to absorb a strong shock on foreign credit flows which provoked a financial crisis in 1995. In the sharp recovery that followed, the reputation of the convertibility regime was much enhanced. But the long process of economic recession, price deflation, deepening fiscal problems and mounting financial restrictions which started in 1998, in a tougher external environment, eventually led to the collapse of the monetary and financial systems. The devaluation at the beginning of 2002 formalized the end of convertibility, in the midst of a crisis that put into question basic aspects of the economic organization of the country.

The deep economic crisis of Argentina has been causing an active quest for conclusions of topical or general importance (and some of this search is conducted and reported live and direct by assorted commentators and analysts). Indeed, an experience of this kind is likely to generate useful lessons for macroeconomic theory and policy design. Some of them may be simple and straightforward (for example, under strong uncertainty, the arguments for precautionary savings should apply particularly to fiscal policies). However, we believe that, despite the temptation to produce instant analysis that may be encapsulated in one-liners (or self-confident exhortations: reform now!, dollarize this way!, float that way![1]) the questions raised hardly lend themselves to trivial answers. In this chapter, we propose to undertake a brief (and certainly partial and preliminary) discussion of the problems related to the design and administration of a monetary regime in an economy such as that of Argentina; in the last section, we refer to the regional spillovers generated within the MERCOSUR area. The ultimate aim is to present arguments that may be of practical use. But we do not intend to push forward a particular prescription, or to analyze in depth the available alternatives. Rather, our interest is to try to discuss conditions and parameters which can affect the choice of monetary policies in what seems to be a rather complex case.

2.   GENERAL ISSUES RELEVANT TO ARGENTINA: SOME COMMENTS

There is an enormous literature that deals with the properties of monetary and exchange rate regimes. Some of it raises issues that are particularly significant for the Argentine case and, at the same time, the Argentine experience poses questions of analytical interest which go beyond the concern for one particular episode. Certainly, we cannot discuss in any detail either that literature or the characteristics of the Argentine economy that may condition choices on monetary matters. However, a brief reference to both is in order. This section contains brief remarks on some general themes which appear prominent when approaching the Argentine case.

2.1   The Context of Monetary and Exchange Rate Policies

In many instances, starting an analysis of monetary policies with a reminder of the elementary 'functions of money' may well be considered a profitless excursion. Normally, one can take for granted the existence of a functioning system of transactions based on the circulation of the national currency and (perhaps with less emphasis) it can be assumed that the broad features of the financial sector will remain under the *ceteris paribus* clause. Most analytical models are naturally built under those presumptions, and the same applies to practical discussions. However, there are cases where the basic elements of a monetary economy are on the table. Hyperinflations question the survival of money as price denominator, and even as means of exchange. In certain economic crises, large-scale bankruptcies may create the danger of almost a complete stop in credit flows. The recent Argentine episode exemplifies how an extreme perturbation may disrupt institutions that provide basic frameworks for financial contracts and routine transactions. When that limit is reached, the problem for policies is, with the instruments at hand, to reconstruct a monetary system, starting from the provision of viable mediums of payment, the management of the currency in such a way that it may serve as unit of account at least for cash prices and short-run credit, and the establishment of conditions in which rudimentary forms of financing may emerge once again. Even that may be a difficult task.

Under less extraordinary circumstances, monetary policies have clearly

more delimited goals. However, in the discussions on monetary issues (particularly those of a practical sort) it often seems difficult to identify what is the
specific set of roles that monetary policies are supposed to have, and how the
potential trade-offs between multiple objectives are assumed to be determined
and weighed in decisions. Monetary and exchange rate systems (as, clearly,
neither can be treated separately) may serve a variety of purposes such as
defining a nominal anchor for price-setting and the denomination of financial
contracts, helping to maintain financial stability (and prevent or handle crises),
contributing to macroeconomic management, and especially to smooth cyclical swings, facilitating the adjustment of the economies to shocks which
require shifts in the real exchange rate, or promoting the growth of trade, in
particular within regional areas.[2]

Some of the restrictions that policy makers face are of a quite general
nature. For example, the tension between the desired degree of autonomy of
monetary policies, the desired degree of openness of the capital account and
the desired degree of exchange rate stability has been much studied as a
'macroeconomic trilemma' (Eichengreen, 1999; Frankel, 1999). But, in any
case, the analysis of the properties of different monetary systems is an intri-
cate matter, which makes it necessary to introduce (perhaps implicit) assumptions about the sets of models which are considered admissible, the institutions
and parameters which characterize the economy and the instruments that
policy makers have at their disposal. Especially when considering a case like
that of Argentina, it seems important to try to contemplate the general context
of the problem, and the ways in which it conditions the analysis; otherwise,
there is a risk of oversimplifying and of biasing not only the 'normative
discussion' of policy alternatives, but also the 'positive' representation of the
reasons for observed past choices.

A central consideration regards the instruments other than monetary policies that the government is able and willing to use. Fiscal conditions which
make governments avid for seigniorage revenues are of course the primary
source of high inflations; pressures on public finances can arise (and there is
ample historical evidence) from problems in the financial sector. The demands
on fiscal policies in order to sustain monetary stability may vary widely from
case to case: with a strong demand for government debt (bonds and money),
the 'unpleasant monetarist arithmetic' (in the celebrated expression of Sargent
and Wallace, 1981) will play itself over long periods, and leave time for
adjustments that may contemplate with some care the effects on allocation and
distribution of alternative fiscal measures. In other cases, the dilemma
adjust/(hyper)inflate is posed over very short horizons (certainly, in association with deep doubts about the solvency of the government), and the urgent
tensions between the requirement of avoiding deficits that cannot be financed
without printing money and the pressures that act on public spending and

revenues are likely to worsen the quality of fiscal policies, with repercussions on monetary credibility. The lack of appropriate instruments, either because of insufficient administrative resources or through an inability to arrange a polit-ical agreement behind systematic policies, greatly restricts the opportunities for a steady monetary management. However, there may be effects in the other direction. The link between 'tight money' and the burden of the public debt is a particularly clear example, but there can be others. In Argentina, for instance, the large perceived exit costs of the fixed exchange rate system directed towards fiscal policies the pressures to improve the competitiveness of the tradable-goods-producing sector in a way that created a tension between the requirements of fiscal prudence and external balance.

The choice of a monetary regime has clearly a relevance that goes far beyond the determination of nominal variables, since it can be expected to influence the 'real' performance of the economy. The 'fiscal' aspects of mone-tary policies themselves imply a non-neutrality, associated with the behavior of seigniorage revenues and the effects on the demand for money. It is gener-ally agreed, however, that the significance of the monetary system would be rather limited in a world of complete markets, common knowledge of the economy's working model and full price flexibility (cf., for example, Obstfeld and Rogoff, 1996, esp. p. 605). But the extension and depth of markets, the features of expectations-formation processes and the characteristics of price-setting practices are likely to vary between economies. This observation would lead to arguments stressing that there is no single monetary or exchange rate system that would be right for all countries at all times (cf. Frankel, 1999). Thus, the analysis should take into account the structure of the economy under study, and also the fact that the monetary regime is among the central deter-minants of economic behavior patterns, so that these cannot be considered as exogenously given when examining policy alternatives.

The literature on monetary and exchange rate policies in developing coun-tries has often emphasized the limited flexibility of nominal prices (see Basu and Taylor, 1999), to the point of arguing that 'deviations from PPP are always and everywhere a monetary phenomenon' (Taylor, 2000). Indeed, there is ample evidence that flexible exchange rate systems generate more short-run variability in real exchange rates, and numerous examples (Argentina among them) illustrate the difficulties that economies face in producing a real devalu-ation under fixed exchange rates. However, real effects on real exchange rates appear to be potentially quite important (and one is left to wonder whether the wide swings in the average incomes in dollar terms of a country like Argentina can be simply attributed to monetary shocks). Moreover, perfect price flexibil-ity does not eliminate the adjustment problems of an economy with nominal contracting, and similarly with floating exchange rates when financial contracts are denominated in foreign currencies. The traditional debt-deflation theme

(Fisher, 1933), which stresses the effects of price movements on the net worth of debtors, and through that, on the supply of credit, has regained prominence in recent discussions, as attention has turned again to the role of monetary policies in financial crises (see Easterly, Islam and Stiglitz, 2000; Mishkin, 2001). The Argentine case has shown in a particularly dramatic form the potential strength of balance sheet effects both in the development of 'twin' financial and currency crises, and in their repercussions on real activity.

Another point concerns model uncertainty. Recent literature has incorporated the fact (quite obvious, notwithstanding the widespread acceptance of the rational expectations assumption) that there is no precise knowledge about a definite and unique model that would generate the evolution of the macroeconomic variables of interest (see, for example, Taylor, 1999; Hansen and Sargent, 2001). Although this makes the analysis more difficult,[3] the complication is indeed a part of the policy problem, and its recognition leads us to realize the convenience that policy recommendations be robust with respect to changes in how the model of the economy is specified (Hansen and Sargent, 2000; von zur Muehlen, 1982, Heymann, 1990). The uncertainty about the specification of the 'right' model and about the quantitative value of parameters can be expected to be particularly intense in economies undergoing transitions, because of policy reforms or other reasons. In the specific instance of Argentina, on several occasions agents had to revise their perceptions of 'what kind of country they live in' (the next section presents some illustrations). Under those circumstances, 'structural parameters' are likely to change, and, at the same time, their identification will be made more difficult by the behavioral adjustments that take place as agents learn to operate in a new environment. This issue, it should be stressed, does not derive simply from a methodological argument (be it a concern for 'realism', or for logical consistency), but from the concrete problems that arise in the design and implementation of monetary policies in 'fluid' conditions. It may be noted, in this regard, that in states where agents are engaged in a particularly intense learning about their opportunities, the demand for flexibility will be consequently strong. From the point of view of monetary policies, this would imply that strong unconditional commitments would have high costs (for example it would be dangerous to establish a hard peg with much uncertainty about the 'sustainable real exchange rate'). But it may well happen that at the same time there is a strong demand on the government to provide an anchor to expectations by defining explicit and easily understandable 'rules of the game', and this may mean that clearly specified restrictions on policies may also be highly valued. Handling the trade-off is likely to create a tough decision problem.

The characteristics of the financial system clearly influence the set of instruments available to monetary policies and the nature and intensity of the problems that it has to deal with. At the same time, the monetary regime strongly conditions financial decisions. The Argentine experience from hyper-inflation to convertibility to the breakdown of convertibility makes the connection apparent. The perception of an extreme monetary instability causes a sharp contraction of the time length of financial contracts and reduces the volume of financial transactions. In hyperinflation, there is no 'natural' unit of account to contract: nominal units have highly uncertain future real values, volatile inflation rates also create risks in indexed contracts, and swings in the real exchange rate induce volatility in the purchasing power of foreign curren-cies. Financial markets 'undevelop', as agents refuse to bear the high risks of making or accepting promises of future payment. The possibilities for produc-tion and consumption consequently shrink; but in such conditions, financial crises are not a first-order matter, since the initial value of (domestic) liabili-ties is already small. By contrast, in a system like that of an established convertibility scheme, the existence of a well-defined and highly visible anchor for expectations greatly contributes to increase the propensity to lend and borrow and thus facilitates economic activity. But if, as is sometimes the case (and it definitely was in Argentina), most debt contracts are 'dollarized', the expansion of credit may be based in part on the illusion that dollar contracting fixes at the same time the foreign currency value of claims and the domestic real value of obligations. In that instance, it may be as if the mone-tary system 'promises too much', by fostering the belief that a hard peg to a certain currency can be sufficient to stabilize the level of incomes denomi-nated in that currency. Here, if agents come to underestimate the risks they take (which, by the way, are hard to determine *ex ante* in an economy under-going a regime change), and are eventually disappointed, the result may be a crisis, and the 'discredit' of the financial system.

One finds here in a particular form a problem related to the incompleteness of contracts. A system like convertibility certainly helps to widen the spectrum of existing financial contracts in comparison with hyperinflation. Asset dollar-ization protects agents against a particular type of shock: a situation where, say, the government 'repudiates its commitments' and produces a more or less neutral inflation (maybe in an attempt to collect more seigniorage). However, the real value of contractual payments will vary widely when the real exchange rate shifts for some reason or other. Insulating obligations from both nominal shocks and real exchange rate 'surprises' would require a richer (or different) set of contracts. If such instruments do not emerge, and individuals keep their focus on the 'inflation risk', then the contractual system would be very vulnerable to exchange rate movements. This, in turn, would influence the incentives for the government by inducing 'fear of floating' (Calvo and Reinhart, 2000). But, if in the end there is after all a sizeable real devaluation, the system of dollarized contracts is likely to break down. In those circum-stances, concerns about the preservation of property rights are no doubt in order, but exhortations in that sense may beg the question of how these rights should be defined when the contingency that has been realized is precisely the one the parties 'chose to be silent about' when making the contract.

Crises can be very traumatic events. It is reasonable that great precautions be taken to avoid them. But it does not logically follow that the chances of ending in a crisis situation should be eliminated, or at least minimized at all costs. In a case like that of Argentina (for the sake of the argument, we are advancing this proposition as one of those 'stylized facts' based on a couple of observations), it proved quite difficult to have at the same time a more or less flexible, non-appreciated exchange rate and actively functioning financial markets. If this apparent trade-off is taken as given, it does not seem trivial at first glance to define what should be the 'acceptable' probability of a crisis that would compensate for the prospective benefits of a fluid supply of credit (and the probability of a crisis seems hardly identifiable in an 'objective' way). One may well wish for much prudence in policy decisions, but how to handle that choice does not look like a foregone conclusion. Of course, it would be very desirable to avoid such difficult trade-offs, like many economies have in fact managed to do. But depending on the initial conditions, this may require a big effort of imagination and skill in policy making.

2.2   Dealing with Shocks and Gaining Credibility

Posing a decision problem for monetary policies in a setting without disturbances or uncertainty is almost a contradiction in terms. And, in any case, the answer would be trivial and straightforward: announce the policy sequence that you always knew was the optimal one (and state it a non-contingent rule: it does no harm and it may do good to make a commitment). The traditional analysis of monetary policies dealt in a central way with the properties of policy systems from the point of view of the stabilization of real activity in economies subject to disturbances. The resulting arguments were that fixed exchange rates are superior to floating rates when the dominant source of shocks is money demand, while flexible rates are appropriate when shocks are mostly of a real type. In the context of developing countries, that distinction seemed too simplified. It was observed that many countries which adopted fixed exchange rates were mostly concerned with the effects (notably on anti-inflationary credibility) of establishing a nominal anchor, and less with short-term stabilization of activity levels. It was also observed that in a context of open capital accounts 'credibly fixed rates may not be a viable long-run option for most countries, given the pervasive possibility of speculative attacks' (Obstfeld and Rogoff, 1996). According to Fischer (2000), 'all the massive crises of the past five years – the really big ones – have been associated with the collapse of formally fixed or quasi-fixed exchange rate systems' (p. 223). This observation has led to the argument for a 'bi-polar' approach, with either a very hard peg or a float. However, there remains influential support for inter-mediate regimes (see Ocampo, 2001; Williamson, 2001).

From an analytical point of view, there appear to be no definite, clear-cut recommendations. It has been mentioned (although of course, the statement should be duly qualified in a discussion made from an Argentine perspective) that the property of being 'crisis free' does not necessarily make a policy regime superior to any alternative (in the same way that, in general, a good investment project need not have a zero probability of bankruptcy). More specifically, Frankel (1999) argues that both floating and fixed exchange rate regimes may be subject to instabilities, in the form of currency overvaluation and large volatility. In turn, the costs and benefits of different alternatives will depend on features of the economy such as the degree of development of financial instruments that may contribute to hedge risk. For instance, the potential effects of exchange rate volatility on trade and investment are likely to be stronger where forward markets or trade in derivatives cannot be used for that purpose, which is often the case in developing economies (Fanelli and Medhora, 2001).

The use of financial contracts to diversify risks derived from shocks such as movements in world commodity prices is also limited. Consequently, national income and consumption are more variable than they may otherwise be (Athanasoulis, Shiller and van Wincoop, 1999; Obstfeld and Rogoff, 2000; Agénor, McDermott and Prasad, 1999). In fact, it has been observed that the volatility of consumption of Latin American economies is strikingly high (IADB, 1995; Fanelli, 2000), which suggests that the degree of international diversification was small.[4] Also, while consumption is less volatile than GDP in many countries, the opposite is observed in Latin America (Fanelli, 2000). Investment volatility also tends to be higher in the Latin American countries, although the difference with developed countries is less marked than in the case of consumption.

The association between international market failures and macroeconomic fluctuations suggests that countercyclical policies and institutional arrange-ments should take into account the potential for cross-country 'mutual insur-ance'. National, regional and multilateral institutions may have comparative advantages for performing different types of countercyclical functions. Notwithstanding the natural concentration of policy makers in Argentina (and its neighbors) in coping somehow with the ongoing crisis, and the absence of an international institutional framework, the exploration of possible forms of regional cooperation to moderate real instability is likely to remain an impor-tant issue.

In any case, 'emerging' economies are likely to face large real shocks, which in some cases may endanger the solvency of resident debtors. If the bonds issued by some countries offer (in normal times) returns as large as those of equity, it may be expected that occasionally they show difficulties in repaying, perhaps to the point of falling into open default. When perceptions about the potential growth rates of an economy are subject to large swings (at times, going from images of 'economic miracles' to those of 'disaster cases' in a few years), optimism may lead to decisions that, while made with expectations that may have seemed down-to-earth and realistic at the time, may very well look after the fact like wild gambles. In the specific case of Argentina, the data shown in the next section suggest that it was indeed quite difficult for agents to project the trend of output and incomes.

In such circumstances, there appears to be no guarantee that risk will be priced appropriately. Bad news can lead to major revisions of beliefs about the economy's future, inducing flight-to-quality behavior by asset holders. One immediate consequence will be that the country will face a sudden worsening in credit market conditions and will experience a tightening in liquidity constraints, amplified and propagated by the effects of economic contraction on net worth, which are fed back into a reduced credit supply (Bernanke, Gertler and Gilchrist, 1983; Bernanke and Gertler, 1995).

In a world of imperfect contract enforcement and limited information, reputation is quite valuable. Consequently, the authorities will have a strong incentive to meet the country's obligations. If interest rates are unusually high or the country is rationed out of credit markets, the response may be to induce or to allow a temporary increase in the real exchange rate, so as to generate trade surpluses in order to meet the external constraint, and in so doing, signal that the country simply experiences liquidity problems. Depreciation of the currency, in this sense, may be assimilated to the behavior of an individual firm which decides to liquidate inventories at a price below cost just to honor bank debt and preserve the value of its reputational capital. However, in some cases, this strategy for preserving 'external' reputation may seem very costly to monetary policies, particularly if they have at stake their credibility for sound, low-inflation behavior, and the financial sector is highly dollarized. Clearly, Argentina has been one of these cases.

Economic policy making confronts incentive problems leading to opportunistic behavior, as well as shocks on the economy that may require 'flexible' actions. The analysis of policy games has generated a large and varied literature. But a caricature of some applied policy advices may look perhaps as a prescription of the kind: 'Be flexible and credible, not rigid or discretionary'. Direct and full of common sense, except for the fact that what once seemed a 'sensible rule' to gain credibility may suddenly be perceived as a straitjacket which impedes an effective response to a shock, or an 'escape clause' meant to retain some flexibility, may appear to some as an open door for discretion that the country pays dearly with high interest rates. There does not seem to be an escape from trying to deal with the trade-offs in the terms in which they present themselves.

In this regard, some quite simple propositions seem uncontroversial:

(a) Since it is not possible to identify and to implement an 'optimal contingent rule' for monetary and exchange rate policy, a first-best arrangement is unattainable.

(b) Decisions regarding monetary institutions will have to consider, explicitly or implicitly, trade-offs which are to some extent economy-specific. There is no general presumption that the same arrangement will fit different economies. In particular, countries may vary considerably with respect to the strength of the potential policy credibility problems *vis-à-vis* the likely intensity of real shocks, and with respect to features of their financial systems which can influence the opportunities and instruments available for monetary policies.

(c) In principle, choices about monetary systems should weigh costs and benefits that will accrue over time. This implies that 'rates of time discount' can have strong effects on the relevant decisions, as the time profile of gains and losses from the policy makers' point of view may vary significantly for different arrangements. In addition, the choice must rely on some evaluation of the nature and characteristics of possible disturbances and about the model(s) that may represent the economy's evolution. Consequently, the decisions may depend on attitudes towards risk and perceptions of dangers and opportunities. In any case, alternatives that were originally preferred may be made inappropriate by some 'atypical' shock or simply by learning from experience: *ex ante* and *ex post* policy evaluations may well be different. Also, some regimes can have (by design or by chance) high 'exit costs'. The irreversible decisions to give up such institutional frameworks can then be 'rationally' delayed, even if the *status quo* is no longer considered the best option.

3. THE ARGENTINE EXPERIENCE

The previous discussion emphasized matters such as the existence of conflicting goals and lack of instruments, model uncertainty, the role of debt-deflation processes, and the complexities of risk management and credibility problems. Such issues appear to be relevant to Argentina, in ways that the following arguments try to illustrate.

3.1 Trends, Shocks and Fluctuations

In 1980, the per capita nominal GDP of Argentina, valued at the ongoing exchange rate and 'inflated' by the increase in the CPI of the USA from that year to 2000, exceeded US$14 000. The economy was then running a trade deficit, so that the per capita domestic absorption was even higher. After the sharp recession and real devaluation that followed the crisis at the beginning of the 1980s, a similar measure of per capita GDP fell to about US$4000 in 1982. In the hyperinflationary environment of 1989, aggregate per capita output fell below U$S3000, and spending dropped even lower. Throughout the recovery, with exchange rate real appreciation which took place under the convertibility regime, the value of GDP rose to above US$9000 per capita in 1994, once again, together with a sizable trade deficit. In the deflationary recession of 1998–2001, the GDP indicator steadily declined, but maintained comparatively high levels (still more than US$7000 dollars in 2001). The devaluation of early 2002 in some sense closed a cycle, as per capita GDP went back to values comparable to those of the early 1980s (see Figure 8.1).

Such wide swings do not simply indicate that the economy showed a strong

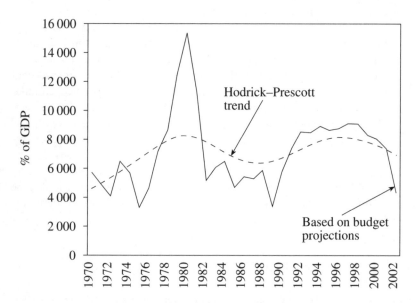

Note: [a] Nominal per capita GDP/exchange rate multiply US CPI.

Figure 8.1   Argentina: GDP per capita (constant dollars of 2000)[a], 1970–2002

'medium-term' volatility, but they also point to a serious problem for the decision making of agents: there was (*ex post*) ample chance that plans based on estimates of individual or aggregate 'sustainable' incomes would be disappointed. Standard measures of trends paint quite different pictures depending on the time period covered by the data. For example, with information up to 1989, the Hodrick–Prescott trend of dollar per capita GDP for that year would have been estimated slightly above 4000, with negative slope; the trend measure for 1989 calculated using data that include the 1990s has a value clearly over US$6000. Using hindsight, an individual could have found that in the late 1980s he had underestimated the permanent purchasing power of income in dollar terms. By 1998, the trend could have looked solid: the Hodrick–Prescott calculation showed a value over U$S9000, and an upward slope. Perhaps, numerous agents may have found tenable the notion that economic reforms were placing the economy on a catching-up path. By 2000, the trend had flattened out: the evolution of the 1990s could have looked more like a change in levels than in the growth rate. Two years later, that level itself seemed highly overestimated: in fact, with data that took into account the devaluation, the whole period of convertibility showed a trend well below the actual values of GDP in dollar terms, and substantially lower than the realized values of domestic spending.

Clearly, there is no reason to assign behavioral meaning to a formula for interpolating data. However, the problem of identifying permanent incomes was indeed there, and could not be bypassed when making decisions dealing with production, spending and asset holding. In addition, the problem did not arise only from relative price (real exchange rate) movements, but from the changes in the volume of GDP itself: the conventional trend measure shows a well-defined downward turning point in the late 1990s, after a sharp increase during that decade (see Figure 8.2). In Argentina, extrapolating past trends has proved to be a hazardous activity.

The difficulty in determining sustainable levels of spending can significantly affect the quality of decisions (see Heymann, Kaufman and Sanguinetti, 2001): with a shifting trend, agents may learn at some point that their expenditures have been in fact highly procyclical and that they had been 'living beyond their means' (negating the perception at the time when the decisions were taken). In Argentina, the realization that wealth estimates had been exaggerated has caused an extremely traumatic adjustment. This was made even more painful by the fact that the system of mostly dollarized financial contracts developed under the convertibility monetary regime was highly vulnerable if the dollar value of incomes fell well short of expectations, and, in turn, the breakdown of contracts was itself a source of economic disorganization.

A country with fluid access to international credit markets where the appropriate assets are traded may be able to diversify a good deal of its idiosyncratic

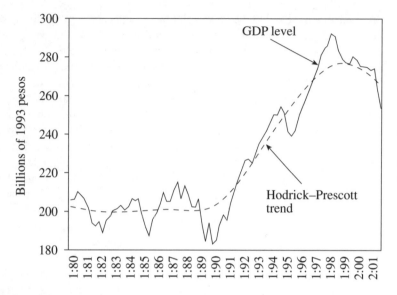

*Figure 8.2   Argentina: GDP 1980–2001 (first quarter data, seasonally
            adjusted)*

risks and to redistribute the effects of shocks across time and states of nature.
But, for Argentina, the volatility of consumption has been very large, and
larger than the volatility of output; moreover, there was no correlation between
its consumption that of the world economy, proxied by that of the USA
(Fanelli, 2000). In recent years, credit market conditions have been visibly
associated with the performance of the Argentine economy, as can be seen in
the co-variation between real GDP and an indicator of 'country risk' (see
Figure 8.3). Clearly, there may be causation in both directions (since risk
premia incorporated in interest rate spreads will depend on the perspectives of
the economy), and it is conceivable that, in general, the correlation between
output and interest rates be either positive or negative (as the driving impulse
may come from the demand side or the supply side of credit markets). But, in
any case, it seems undeniable that the tightening of financial constraints was
one of the main elements in the drastic fall in aggregate demand and output in
the long Argentine recession still under way.

When it is not easy to smooth the effects of shocks, monetary policies face
stronger dilemmas. Tighter liquidity constraints induce financial accelerator
effects which tend to accentuate cyclical fluctuations and to generate financial
instability. Such disturbances can be particularly strong when capital inflows
are liable to experience sudden stops (Calvo, Izquierdo and Talvi, 2002). As
foreign finance contracts, the pressure mounts in the foreign exchange market.

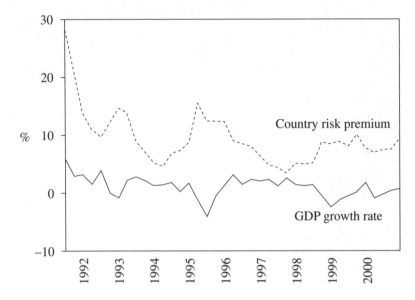

Figure 8.3   Argentina: country risk premium and growth rate, 1992–2000 (%)

The link between capital flows, foreign reserves and the exchange rate is a source of tension for any monetary system and, under certain circumstances, may induce a regime change.

3.2   The Real Exchange Rate: Variability and Regime Shifts

In trying to identify a 'sustainable' real exchange rate, one searches for a relative price that would be compatible with intertemporal equilibrium, given the economy's future opportunities and performance. Not a trivial matter, to say the least. In Argentina, both analysts and economic agents have faced problems in going about the task. The series of the real exchange rate of the Argentine currency with respect to the US dollar has shown high volatility and several breaks (see Fanelli and Rozada, 1998). Typically, sharp upward jumps were followed by periods of strong variability (see Figure 8.4). Such jumps coincided with the sudden ends of currency pegs of some type or other, after balance of payments crises with significant capital flight. Such regime changes (in 1975, 1981, 1989 and 2001) were associated with major swings in economic policies. The two periods of lowest volatility in the series correspond to systems where the exchange rate was used as the nominal anchor: the 'tablita' 1978–81 and the decade of convertibility (1991–2001).

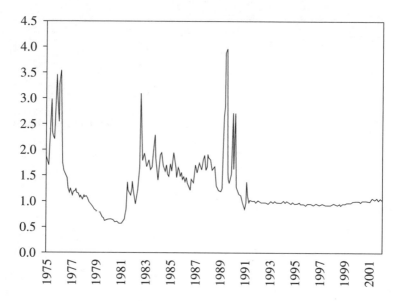

Figure 8.4   Real exchange rate (WPI), USA/Argentina, 1975–2001

Movements in the real exchange rate have been highly correlated with shifts in the nominal exchange rate (Fanelli, 2001). Thus, here too, domestic price adjustments have contributed comparatively little (relative to the nominal exchange rate) to the variations in the real exchange rate (Rogoff, 1996; Froot and Rogoff, 1995; Basu and Taylor, 1999). Different degrees of price inertia may imply that disinflation processes take place with significant movements in relative prices (which can generate 'entry costs' for such policies). In Argentina, disinflations have usually taken place together with real appreciations, although the large increases in domestic demand that were observed in some cases (notably, the start of the convertibility system) suggest that this was not simply the result of frictions in price-setting.

Anyhow, in the initial period of the convertibility regime, the inflation rate was higher than the international levels, which resulted in a sizeable price increase before a definite stabilization occurred (the CPI rose 60 per cent between March 1991 and December 1996, while the WPI increased 20 per cent). This was associated with a significant real appreciation. In the second half of the 1990s, the currency depreciated in real terms against the dollar as Argentine prices stopped growing, and later fell in nominal terms during the recession until the end of 2001. However, this gradual and 'incremental' effect was offset by the revaluation of the currency (along with the dollar) with respect to the euro and, particularly, the Brazilian real.

During the 1990s, the transmission of macroeconomic impulses between the countries of MERCOSUR grew more important as the volume of trade expanded, starting from quite low levels. In consequence, the bilateral real exchange with Brazil became an increasingly significant variable for Argentina. Fanelli (2001) examined the properties of the series using GARCH models. This study found a large volatility in the variable, with strong effects of regime changes such as the launching of the Argentine convertibility in 1991 and the floating (*cum* devaluation) of the Brazilian currency in 1999. In the case of developed countries, the purchasing power parity (PPP) property does not hold in the short run, but seems to apply after a long adjustment period; there is no evidence of this behavior for developing countries, due to lack of data (Froot and Rogoff, 1995; Edwards and Savastano, 1999). In the case of Argentina and Brazil (maybe because of the comparatively weaker price inertia in economies with inflationary experience), the variance around the mean is larger than for other economies, but deviations have smaller mean durations. In fact, the presence of a unit root is rejected more easily for the Argentina–Brazil bilateral real exchange rate than it is for the exchange rates of developed countries (Fanelli, 2001). That is, the historical experience has been one where the bilateral exchange rate has varied a great deal, but does not seem to have a 'permanent' drift. This result may be relevant when examining the possibilities of monetary cooperation within MERCOSUR after the current crisis has passed one way or the other.

3.3   Financial Intermediation

A number of studies found that financial constraints have been particularly strong in Argentina, even during periods where the supply of credit was fluid by the country's standards (Fanelli and Keifman, 2002; Bebczuk, 2000; Schmuckler and Vesperoni, 2000; Bebczuk, Fanelli and Pradelli, 2002). This research suggests that: (i) credit markets have been very markedly segmented; (ii) firms are to a great extent financed with retained earnings, and the volume of cash flows influences strongly investment decisions; (iii) the capital structure of firms varies much with the macroeconomic environment; (iv) changes in the volume of credit anticipate movements in real activity; and (v) movements in 'country risk' indicators are strongly related to domestic financial variables (for example one percentage point increase in that index was associated on average with a 2.2 fall in the value of firms whose shares trade in the Argentine stock market).

Lack of depth, instability and dollarization marked the evolution of financial intermediation in Argentina in the last decades. Under convertibility, higher integration with the world economy and price stability changed the behavior with respect to that observed in previous periods, but the expansion and diversification of financial activity proved to be transitory. In the 1990s, the demand for domestic financial assets increased significantly as a share of GDP, but it was quite variable, and very dependent on external conditions, with large shocks associated with events like the Mexican devaluation, the Russian episode of 1998 and, later on, the strong skepticism of international operators about the future of the local economy. Also, the degree of dollarization of the domestic financial system increased. In the end, the process of erosion of the financial system that started in the last part of the past decade escalated in 2001 into an extremely deep crisis, which seems likely to have lasting consequences, and to leave the economy with quite undeveloped credit markets.

This crisis was a particularly extreme episode in a history of large changes in financial conditions, which were reflected in indicators like the leverage ratios of firms and the relative share of short- and long-run debt in total financing. Typically, in times of scarce supply of funds, firms tend to issue short-term debt, or liquidate assets in order to cushion the effects of credit crunches and try to reduce their financial obligations, while in 'tranquil' periods, leverage levels tend to increase, and more long-term financing is utilized. In this regard, it has been a feature of the Argentine economy that most assets with more than a few months' duration (or less, depending on circumstances) have been denominated in dollars. This characteristic, which of course derives from the uncertainties of agents about the future of the economy, particularly with respect to monetary management (and, in the 1990s, was probably also influenced to some extent by legal restrictions to price indexation), has implied that an expansion of longer-run credit (of either external or internal origin) carried with it the risk of currency mismatches if the exchange rate varied significantly.

Typically in Argentina, when macroeconomic conditions worsen, creditors react by shifting their demand towards dollarized assets with short-term maturities. The shortening of duration can be linked to a desire to monitor more closely the performance of debtors, and to the fact that uncertainty raises liquidity premia. If the duration of the assets of firms does not vary much, then their financial position deteriorates, and default becomes more likely. This, in turn, reduces the supply of credit as it is perceived by prospective lenders. Such effects are consistent with the cyclical evolution of the balance sheets of Argentine firms. A macroeconomic consequence is that economic downturns are associated with pressures on both financial and exchange markets. When the disturbance is strong enough, it may end in 'twin crises'.

Problems of liquidity and duration mismatch can be linked to the behavior of risk management by banks, and to certain features of prudential regulations (see Calomiris and Powell, 2000; Fanelli and Medhora, 2001). In Argentina, the experience has been that, when the level of perceived systemic risk increases, banks hedge against currency risk and seek a better matching of the duration of assets and liabilities. This behavior puts financial pressure on business firms, and can lead to higher counter-party risk. Risk tends to migrate in the financial system because hedging does not reduce systemic risk: it transfers the exposure elsewhere or transforms the type of the exposure from currency or interest rate risk to credit risk (see Kimbal, 2000). The phenomenon of risk migration would qualify the argument that credit contraction in a downturn is a healthy reaction of a banking system subject to market discipline. The current Argentine crisis indicates that when the economy is very weak, transferring risks to their business borrowers may not solve the fragility of banks.

3.4   Credibility and Rules under a Hard Peg

Monetary policies typically face a trade-off between credibility and flexibility. The emphasis varies with the times: high inflation tends to cause great dislike for monetary discretion (with muted calls for flexibility), while depressions give prominence to the problems of rigid systems. The question (which the Argentine case raises in a particularly sharp form) is how to address monetary management in an economy where policy making as a whole has suffered much discredit and where at the same time simple, seemingly unconditional rules have shown their defects (and limited credibility) in the event of large disturbances. What seems clear is that, when strong perceived incentive problems for policy making are combined with potentially large real shocks, what remains is to pick among high-cost alternatives, although the timing of the costs will not necessarily be the same under different choices.

   When the Argentine government decided to implement the convertibility regime the foremost concern was to cut inflation, and there was a widespread conviction that economic disturbances originated from policy malincentives, manifested particularly in lax and erratic monetary policies. Moreover, the salience of the US dollar as a unit of account, savings instrument and even medium of exchange (particularly in large transactions, like those in real estate), was already well established. A tight link to the dollar with strong constraints to monetary discretion was then seen as a mechanism that would discipline policies, by legally eliminating the monetary financing of deficits, and provide a definite anchor for the price system. Dealing with negative real shocks was not a primary consideration and, in any case, arguments to that effect could easily be perceived as subterfuges intended to 're-open the door to monetary discretion'. The fact that under convertibility inflation definitely stopped and the monetary system withstood a shock as large as the 1995 financial crisis greatly enhanced its reputation. In the recovery that followed, convertibility was widely identified with sound policies (to the extent that proposals for policy reform in other areas were given names such as 'fiscal convertibility', or 'social convertibility').

The convertibility regime eventually came to be regarded as one of the country's basic institutions, with a significance that grew beyond the limited areas of monetary policies or even economic matters as such. The confidence in convertibility promoted the growth in the volume of transactions and in the size and depth of financial markets. At the same time, the participants in dollarized credit operations were likely to entertain inconsistent expectations: lenders probably focused on the legal basis of their claims to dollars, while borrowers may have had the perception that in the 'rare' event of a change in regime, their obligations would be renegotiated. The expectations of both sides could only be validated if the exchange rate remained fixed, and (in order to maintain the solvency of debtors) the dollar values of income were growing, or at least more or less steady. Since under convertibility the economy had generated a quite high average level of dollar incomes for a relatively long period of time, the 'adaptive' perception that those incomes could be projected forward may have been strengthened. In any case, the widespread use of the dollar clause suggested that there remained doubts about the future of the monetary system, but interest rate spreads did not indicate a strong skepticism[5] until the recession which ended convertibility was well under way. In turn, the diffusion of dollar contracting vividly increased the costs of leaving convertibility. There was thus a lock-in effect, derived not only from the legal framework but, mainly, from the financial behavior that had been induced under the monetary regime. The implicit 'escape clause' of rules was only to be applied in this case under extreme circumstances, when it had become obvious that the regime was unsustainable. If it had to happen, the exit from convertibility was bound to be a very disruptive event, after a process that closed the options of holding to the system.

The strong reluctance of successive governments (shared by the large majority of public opinion) to even consider removing the dollar anchor after export prices had dropped substantially, the dollar had appreciated against the euro, Brazil had devalued, foreign credit had tightened and the economy was in recession with unemployment well into two digits, and rising, did not come (as sometimes interpreted) from some peculiar preferences with respect to a presumed output–inflation trade-off, but from a concrete fear that devaluation would cause such a disturbance in financial contracts that the effect would be a drastic fall in activity. In fact, apart from cautious suggestions to contemplate a process of monetary convergence with Brazil, the proposals that circulated to modify the monetary regime went rather in the direction of full dollarization. The notion behind those proposals was that the growing troubles of the Argentine economy were due to concerns about possible policy tampering with the monetary system. In that argument, a further tightening of the monetary rule

(such that the tie to the dollar was seen as irreversible) would signal a commitment to sound policies, and induce a fall in 'country risk' indices, and a revival
of activity. The assumption was that if only that signal could be sent (and
maybe, also, policies were to be disciplined by strengthening the monetary
regime) the level of dollar incomes could, it was hoped, be sustained, with the
contribution of a renewed wave of capital inflows. The 'external constraint'
(which made the credit structure vulnerable in instances were the equilibrium
real exchange rate was noticeably higher that the going value) and the possibility that dollarization also had an implicit 'escape clause' were left out of the
picture.

Convertibility was meant, among other purposes, as an instrument to
constrain fiscal policies. However, persistent deficits, especially after the 1994
reform of the social security system (which does not seem to have been interpreted in Ricardian fashion by the public and by asset holders), caused a
continuous increase in public debt. Whether the performance of fiscal policies
was mostly due to problems of incentives (like those which for years have
complicated the financial relationship between the national government and
the provinces) or to the belief that future growth would provide the funds to
repay the debts is a moot point here. When the economy went into recession,
fiscal policies were burdened with a variety of demands: they had to contemplate the increasing skepticism of creditors, which was causing visible rises in
the cost of financing (before it led to a complete closure of the access to new
funds), the claims for social spending, and the mounting concerns about the
competitiveness of tradable-goods-producing sectors while tax revenues were
falling. As the exchange rate was unavailable to deal with the external adjustment, the government was urged to compensate the observed loss of competitiveness as deflation and reduced real activity operated to lower taxation. In
the end, the credit constraint became the foremost worry, and the authorities
decided to adopt a 'cash rule' where payments of the public sector for primary
expenditures would adjust to receipts. Government salaries and pensions were
reduced (with the understanding that future levels would follow the evolution
of revenues), and tax policies were modified in rapid succession trying to
capture revenues and boost activity. Under a strong economic shock, the
monetary rule was administered together with practically complete discretion
in fiscal policies (which included the delegation of emergency powers in
economic matters to the executive branch). But this did little to restore expectations: by now, the burden of proof rested clearly on those who still expressed
some hope that the collapse could be prevented. 'Country risk' indices showed
that markets assigned a rapidly rising probability to a default. Small local
savers also ran for cover. The quick fall in the demand for deposits started to
put strong pressure on monetary policies themselves, as the central bank inter-
vened to assist the banks with rediscounts, and rapidly lost reserves. The

tensions in fiscal policies grew to the point that several provincial governments started to issue small-denomination bonds which circulated as 'emergency monies'. The 'internal drain' of deposits, combined with the 'external
drain' of foreign reserves, the extreme difficulties of fiscal policies and the
deepening recession, acted jointly to generate explosive economic and social
conditions, where the credibility of the statement that 'one peso equals one
dollar' was quickly vanishing. When the government decided in December
2001 to impose exchange controls and to restrict the withdrawal of funds from
the banks, the convertibility system had in fact been broken. At the beginning
of 2002, a formal devaluation sanctioned the end of the convertibility era,
while the government declared default on its debt.

The episode involved a wholesale breaking of explicit and implicit
contracts, both in the process where policies made a final attempt to sustain
convertibility and avoid explicit default on the public debt, and after the devaluation. In the resulting turmoil, the economic system was devoid of reference
points (as, prominently, convertibility had been for a decade), and fell into a
state of disorganization and severe conflict: in particular, credit transactions
stopped, a final run on the banks was only repressed by a compulsory repro-
gramming of deposits (which did not prevent a considerable monetary expansion) and, while owners of dollar-denominated assets (naturally) held fiercely
to their claims to receive 'actual dollars' and thus loudly rejected 'pessifica-
tion', many debtors resisted the adjustment of their obligations by a CPI-
linked index after they had been transformed into pesos at a one-to-one rate.

The (probably inexorable, in the end) breakdown of the tight monetary rule
of convertibility left the economy without a framework for financial contracting, and monetary policies were thrown into trying to manage a system of dirty
floating lacking a defined institutional setting, in conditions where the demand
for bank deposits or government debt was practically non-existent. The crisis
posed no less a policy problem than to (re-)establish the basic elements of
monetary and financial systems, which had been shattered and discredited.

4.   CONCLUDING REMARKS

By early 2002, the Argentine economy did not have a functioning financial
system and instruments of monetary control were clearly lacking, in a state of
disillusionment and uncertainty such that a demand for foreign currencies
remained strong after a sharp initial devaluation. The disappearance of credit
meant that an aggregate excess supply of money could well coexist with a situation of 'illiquidity' and restricted trades in significant segments of the economy. Given that domestic assets had been redenominated in pesos, the
'political economy' of devaluation possibly changed, as debtors could now

expect to be favored by a depreciation of the currency. Traces of the behavior patterns developed in the 1990s were present in the relatively slow initial response of prices to the jump in the exchange rate. However, the risk that a runaway depreciation would induce agents to dollarize transactions was clearly perceived. There was then a possible scenario where the economy would switch in a short period of time from deflation to a widespread refusal to use the domestic currency. Beyond the immediate concern of economic policies of trying to avoid that outcome, the problem of redefining a monetary regime was urgently posed.

The historical experience shows that Argentina did not find a practical way around the typical dilemmas of monetary management, which were made tougher by the loss of reputation of policies (which favored the dollarization of contracts) and by the difficulty of identifying a useful 'working model' of an economy that often seemed to be in a state of transition. If the design of a monetary regime is not a trivial business even when most other features of the economic system can be left under the *ceteris paribus* umbrella, the complexity of the matter needs not be stressed when that is not the case.

However, some pragmatic principles have a quite general validity. An obvious one is that budgetary control represents a necessary condition for any reasonably stable monetary system to work and be sustained. The need to have a monetary framework with a well-defined institutional status, and objectives which give high priority to slow-moving and predictable prices, is generally well understood. But the monetary regime is only one component of the institutional infrastructure: sooner or later, it will be threatened if fiscal policies do not cooperate to make it viable. Also, it has been amply verified that financial instability can result in large fiscal costs and strong (and possibly unbearable) pressures on monetary management.

In turn, the behavior of the financial system is influenced by the monetary set-up. A well-managed and well-capitalized banking system is a requisite for avoiding financial crises which may jeopardize monetary stability. However, it is not a sufficient condition, since the health of the banking system is dependent on the macroeconomic environment. In the Argentine experience, it has been observed that the financial position of business firms can rapidly deteriorate under unfavorable macroeconomic circumstances. Clearly, when the debtors are vulnerable, the solvency of banks may turn out to be at stake. And the recent Argentine crisis shows how perceptions that banks are solid can gradually be transformed into doubts and eventually change into a distrust that induces a panic withdrawal of deposits. Thus, the macroeconomic properties of a monetary system (including both its institutional credibility and its capacity to help the economy absorb shocks) are ultimately among the main factors in its robustness or fragility. But also, these depend on the presence or absence of ways for the economy to diversify its idiosyncratic risks. The matter has international aspects, at both regional and global levels. Defects in the international 'architecture' may well combine with domestic misperceptions and incentive problems to hinder the development of sound and stable macroeconomic policies.

Historically, Argentina has not managed to establish a monetary system that may combine credibility of a stable performance of nominal variables with flexibility (particularly, in the exchange rate) to deal with shocks. A long experience has greatly damaged the credibility of 'hands-free' policies, while at the same time the economy has experienced extremely large disturbances which demanded policy flexibility of some type or other. The problem was posed in a particularly harsh way in the crisis that led to the end of the convertibility system, and after the devaluation. In the crisis, Argentina was in a way forced to float the currency, an event which was much feared for its potentially destructive effects (which, unfortunately, were observed) on the system of financial contracts. Under the conditions of Argentina after convertibility, the management of monetary policies with a floating exchange rate is very difficult. *De facto* dollarization may be a consequence. Formal dollarization (at some, possibly quite high parity) also presents itself as a possibility, to go along with the argument that 'people only want dollars', and that the chance of keeping a national currency has been lost. However, dollarization does not guarantee (as convertibility did not) stability in aggregate incomes in dollar terms, or in the value of assets: Argentina will not get this just by adopting the US currency. Therefore, the problems of having prices and contracts denominated in a unit of account with a potentially variable value in terms of domestic goods would remain, and probably result again in large macroeconomic fluctuations. Also, after a financial crash and with extreme institutional uncertainty, the most relevant risk is credit risk: prospective lenders care about the denomination of the contract, but are mostly concerned with the perceived low probability that the contract will be honored. It is clear that having a generally acceptable means of exchange and a viable unit of denomination are basic conditions for a functioning economy. It will soon be seen whether the domestic money may serve those purposes. But, in any case, it remains unclear how credit risk would be mitigated and managed with dollarization. Also, the actual unconditional irreversibility of a decision to dollarize may be subject to question.

Once again, in the first months of 2002 there was great uncertainty about the form the monetary system would take, with the possibilities ranging from floating to dollarization, or a new attempt to peg the exchange rate at a higher level. It was easier to indicate the potential problems of each alternative than to specify the preferable option. In any case, the matter had a regional dimension: the effects on MERCOSUR were also to be considered. Clearly, the optimism about the integration process which prevailed in the mid-1990s, when the intra-regional flows of goods were expanding at a very fast rate, was changed later into deep skepticism, with macroeconomic conditions in Argentina and Brazil being the cause of increasing controversies between the participating countries as the volume of trade stagnated. MERCOSUR figured strongly in Argentine perceptions as a source of problems during a good part of the current recession; it lost prominence as the crisis got deeper and attention was concentrated on the pressing and urgent domestic problems, and the view on international matters was focused on the day-to-day signs about attitudes of the USA and the IMF regarding the country's financial troubles. However, the choice of a monetary system is not a matter to approach with an extremely short-run view (although certainly, time horizons tend to shrink dramatically at times of crisis). The performance of the regional neighbors will still have effects on Argentina, and even more after the devaluation has sharply raised the measured degree of openness of the economy. Given the increased importance of exports for Argentina, it may be argued that the possibility of re-starting and developing the integration process may have a high value (Chudnovsky and Fanelli, 2002). At the same time, extreme macroeconomic instability is a serious restriction for any growth-oriented policy, and clearly, the regional role in the treatment of the Argentine crisis appears quite limited (although neighbors have an interest in the recovery of the Argentine economy, among the narrowly economic reasons, because of the size of income effects on trade; see Heymann and Navajas, 1998).

The outcome of the crisis will greatly determine the possibilities that will remain open (or closed) for Argentina in the future. But the option value of getting MERCOSUR moving again seems significant enough to take into account. In this regard, formal dollarization would imply a permanent (in principle) impediment to any form of monetary coordination within the region, and would likely be interpreted as an obstacle to economic integration. With independently floating currencies on its side, bilateral exchange rates are likely to show considerable volatility, and the resulting spillovers may well be a source of friction (as, for instance, it was observed in the episode of the 1999 devaluation of Brazil). If Argentina manages to define a viable monetary–fiscal policy in the immediate future, and moves towards a normalization of the economy, a (certainly long and gradual) process of macroeconomic coordination with Brazil may appear as an interesting possibility, aiming at the establishment of regional macroeconomic standards and the search for strategic goals of policy coordination, particularly in the monetary and financial areas. In the end, if the current crisis is somehow solved, and mechanisms to promote steady and systematic policies and to reduce and diversify risk can be found, MERCOSUR could still be an actor in the international system.

NOTES

*   Paper prepared for the International Conference 'Towards Regional Currency Areas',
    Santiago de Chile, 26–27 March 2002. Comments by Adrián Ramos are gratefully acknowl-
    edged. The opinions expressed in this document are those of the authors and may not neces-
    sarily reflect those of the organizations to which they are affiliated.
1. The tone and the degree of analytical subtlety of some of these pronouncements can be sampled
    in statements like that of Hanke (2002): 'Argentina's devaluation . . . represented more – much
    more – than a garden-variety devaluation. It was a great bank robbery . . . Moral: In a country
    that fails to adhere to the rule of law, the domestic currency should be replaced with a foreign
    currency produced in a country that embraces the rule of law', or that of Krugman (2001): 'Let
    the peso float, and do what is necessary to save the economy . . . Admittedly, the fact that much
    private debt in Argentina is indexed to the dollar means that the peso devaluation might create
    financial problems . . . There is an answer: Simply issue a decree canceling the indexation . . . It
    is more or less what Roosevelt did in 1933.' Recently, Caballero and Dornbusch (2002) have
    made their contribution to the variegated heap of injunctions, by urging Argentina to surrender
    its economic sovereignty into the hands of a foreign expert; they did not care to specify their
    assumptions about which law such expert-ruler would operate under, and about what strength
    (local, external?) would back the enforcement of his/her authority.
2. Cf. for example Turnovsky (1995), Mishkin (1999), Mishkin and Savastano (2000).
3. Some of the difficulties are of a logical nature. For instance, a number of applied exercises
    use the procedure of building different 'rational expectations' models (that is, the expectations
    of agents are supposed to be consistent with the distributions generated by the model), and
    then evaluate policy alternatives (on the basis of some set of preferences over macroeconomic
    outcomes) under the various models, in order to find out which policy courses produce agree-
    able results over a broad enough range of specifications. This method immediately raises a
    logical issue: the analyst is acting as if several models were held to be plausible; the agents
    who 'inhabit' each model are assumed to believe exclusively and with no doubts in that
    particular model. Either the analyst knows more than the agents (about the uncertainty regard-
    ing the true model) or one set of 'models agents' is right and the others, and the analyst, are
    wrong (for different reasons). But, actually, for the exercise to make sense, the agents inhabit
    one and the same economy: how can one 'rational' individual entertain several expectations,
    model-based or not? As (a version of) the saying goes: the analysis may well work in prac-
    tice, but apparently won't do in theory.
4. With diversification, the consumption levels of different countries would be highly correlated
    (Basu and Taylor, 1999). However, in Latin America, the correlation between national and
    world consumption growth (proxied by consumption in USA) is typically lower than the
    correlation between the growth rates of the country and the world economy. In some instances
    (such as that of Argentina), the consumption correlation has actually been negative.
5. Taking into account that part of the spreads could be attributed to a risk premium, given that
    a 'devaluation state' could be expected to be one of low consumption, so that having peso
    debts carried value as a consumption hedge.

REFERENCES

Agénor, P., C.J. McDermott and E.S. Prasad (1999), 'Macroeconomic Fluctuations in
    Developing Countries: Some Stylized Facts', *The World Bank Economic Review*,
    Vol. 14, No. 2, pp. 251–85.
Athanasoulis, S., R. Shiller and E. van Wincoop (1999), 'Macro Markets and Financial
    Security', *FRNBY Economic Policy Review*, April, pp. 21–39.
Basu, S. and A.M. Taylor (1999), 'Business Cycles in International Historical
    Perspective', *Journal of Economic Perspectives*, Vol. 13, Spring, pp. 45–68.

Bebczuk, R. (2000), 'Corporate Saving and Financing Decisions in Argentina', *Economica,* Vol. 5, pp. 1–30.

Bebczuk, R., J.M. Fanelli and J.J. Pradelli (2002), 'Determinants and Consequences of Financial Constraints Facing Firms in Argentina', mimeo, IDB–CEDES.

Bernanke, B. and M. Gertler (1995), 'Inside the black box: the credit channel of monetary transmission', *Journal of Economic Perspectives,* Vol. 9, No. 4, pp. 5–15.

Bernanke, B., M. Gertler and S. Gilchrist (1983), 'The Financial Accelerator and the Flight to Quality', *NBER Working Paper* No. 4789, July.

Caballero, R. and R. Dornbusch (2002), 'Argentina: A Rescue Plan that Works', mimeo, 27 February.

Calomiris, C.W. and A. Powell (2000), 'Can Emerging Market Bank Regulators Establish Credible Discipline? The Case of Argentina, 1992–1999', *NBER Working Paper* No. 7715.

Calvo, G.A. and C.M. Reinhart (2000), 'Fear of Floating', paper prepared for the conference on Currency Unions, Stanford, California.

Calvo, G.A., A. Izquierdo and E. Talvi (2002), 'Sudden Stops, the Real Exchange Rate and Fiscal Sustainability: Argentina's Lessons', background paper for the seminar The Resurgence of Macro Crises: Causes and Implications for Latin America, Forteza, Brazil, 11 March.

Chudnovksky, D. and J.M. Fanelli (2002), *El desafío de integrarse para crecer. Balance de una década de Mercosur,* Madrid: Siglo XXI Editores.

Easterly, W., R. Islam and J.E. Stiglitz (2000), 'Shaken and Stirred: Explaining Growth Volatility', The World Bank.

Edwards, S. and M.A. Savastano (1999), 'Exchange Rates in Emerging Economies: What Do We Need to Know?', *NBER Working Paper* No. 7228.

Eichengreen, Barry (1999), 'Strengthening the International Financial Architecture: Where Do We Stand?', mimeo, University of California Berkeley.

Fanelli, José María (2000), 'Macroeconomic Regimes, Growth and the International Agenda in Latin America', *Latin American Trade Network,* Buenos Aires: Flacso, pp. 5–35.

Fanelli, José María (ed.) (2001), *Coordinación de Políticas Macroeconómicas en el Mercosur,* Madrid: Siglo XXI Editores.

Fanelli, J.M. and M. Rozada (1998), 'Convertibilidad, Volatilidad y Estabilidad Macroeconómica en Argentina', *Estudios de Política Económica y Finanzas,* October.

Fanelli, J.M. and S. Keifman (2002), 'Finance and Changing Trade Patterns in Developing Countries', J.M. in Fanelli and R. Medhora (eds), *Finance and Competitiveness in Developing Countries,* London: Routledge.

Fanelli, J.M. and R. Medhora (2001), 'The Emerging International Financial Architecture and Its Implications for Domestic Financial Architecture', paper presented at the Conference on Domestic Finance and Global Capital in Latin America, organized by the Latin America Research Group, Research Department. Federal Reserve Bank of Atlanta, Miami, Florida, 1–2 November.

Fischer, S. (2000), 'Proposals and IMF Actions to Reduce the Frequency of Crises', in E.S. Rosengren and J.S. Jordan (eds), *Building an Infrastructure for Financial Stability,* Federal Reserve Bank of Boston Conference Series, No. 44, pp. 223–7.

Fisher, I. (1933), 'The Debt Deflation Theory of Great Depressions', *Econometrica,* Vol. 1, pp. 3–21.

Frankel, J.A. (1999), 'No Single Currency Regime is Right for All Countries or at All Times', *NBER Working Paper* No. 7338.

Froot, K.A. and K. Rogoff (1995), 'Perspectives on PPP and Long-run Real Exchange Rate', in G. Grossman and K. Rogoff (eds), *Handbook of International Economics*, vol. III, ch. 32, pp. 1647–88.

Hanke, S. (2002), Testimony, US House of Representatives, Committee on Financial Services, Subcommittee on International Monetary Policy and Trade, 5 March.

Hansen, L. and T. Sargent (2001), 'Acknowledging Misspecification in Macroeconomic Theory', mimeo, University of Chicago.

Heymann, D. (1990), 'Decisiones con Conocimiento Limitado', *Revista de Economía*, August, pp. 22–30.

Heymann, D. and F. Navajas (1998), 'Coordinación de Políticas Macroeconómicas en Mercosur: Algunas Reflexiones', in CEPAL, *Ensayos sobre la inserción regional de la Argentina, Documento de Trabajo No. 81*, Buenos Aires: CEPAL, pp. 35–50.

Heymann, D., M. Kaufman and P. Sanguinetti (2001), 'Learning about Trends: Spending and Credit Fluctuations in Open Economies', in A. Leijonhufvud (ed.), *Monetary Theory as a Basis for Monetary Policy*, Basingstoke: Palgrave.

Inter-American Development Bank (1995), *Economic and Social Progress in Latin America, 1995*, Washington, DC: Inter-American Development Bank.

Kimbal, R. (2000), 'Failures in Risk Management', *New England Economic Review*, January/February, pp. 3–12.

Krugman, P. (2001), 'A Cross of Dollars', *The New York Times*, 7 November.

Mishkin, Frederic S. (1999), 'International Experiences with Different Monetary Policy Regimes', *NBER Working Paper* No. 7044.

Mishkin, Frederic S. (2001), 'Financial Policies and the Prevention of Financial Crises in Emerging Market Countries', *NBER Working Paper* No. 8087.

Mishkin, F.S. and M.A. Savastano (2000), 'Monetary Policy Strategies for Latin America', *NBER Working Paper* No. 7617.

Obstfeld, M. and K. Rogoff (1996), *Foundations of International Macroeconomics*, Cambridge, MA: MIT Press.

Obstfeld, M. and R. Rogoff (2000), 'The Six Major Puzzles in International Macroeconomics: Is There a Common Cause?', *NBER Working Paper* No. 7777.

Ocampo, José Antonio (2001), 'Recasting the International Financial Agenda', mimeo, Santiago, ECLAC.

Rogoff, K. (1996). 'The Purchasing Power Parity Puzzle', *Journal of Economic Literature*, Vol. XXXIV, No. 2, June, pp. 647–68.

Sargent, T. and Neil Wallace (1981), 'Some Unpleasant Monetarist Arithmetic', *Federal Reserve Bank of Minneapolis Quarterly Review*, Winter, pp. 15–31.

Schmuckler, S. and E. Vesperoni (2000), 'Does Integration with Global Markets Affect Firms Financing Choices? Evidence from Emerging Economies', mimeo, Washington, The World Bank.

Taylor, Alan M. (2000), 'A Century of Purchasing Power Parity', *NBER Working Paper* No. 7577.

Taylor, J. (ed.) (1999), *Monetary Policy Rules*, NBER Business Cycle Series, Vol. 31.

Turnovsky, Stephen J. (1995), *Methods of Macroeconomic Dynamics*, Cambridge, MA: MIT Press.

Von zur Muehlen, K. (1982), 'Activist vs Non-Activist Monetary Policy: Optimal Rules under Extreme Uncertainty. A Primer on Robust Control', mimeo, Federal Reserve Board, Washington.

Williamson, John (2001), 'Exchange Rate Policy in Latin America: The Costs of the Conventional Wisdom', mimeo, Institute for International Economics.

Index